D0445233

When It Hits the Fan

When It Hits the Fan

Managing the Nine Crises of Business

Gerald C. Meyers
with
John Holusha

Houghton Mifflin Company
Boston · 1986

Copyright © 1986 by Gerald C. Meyers

All rights reserved. No part of this work may be reproduced or transmitted in any form or by any means, electronic or mechanical, including photocopying and recording, or by any information storage or retrieval system, except as may be expressly permitted by the 1976 Copyright Act or in writing from the publisher. Requests for permission should be addressed in writing to Houghton Mifflin Company, 2 Park Street, Boston, Massachusetts 02108.

Library of Congress Cataloging-in-Publication Data

Meyers, Gerald C.
When it hits the fan.

Includes index.
1. Crisis management.   I. Holusha, John.   II. Title.
HD49.M48   1986   658.4   86-10433
ISBN 0-395-41171-8

Printed in the United States of America

P   10   9   8   7   6   5   4   3

Charts were drawn by Mary Reilly.

To Barbara,
Susan, Andy, and Nancy

Acknowledgments

MANY TOP business leaders have contributed to the thoughts contained in this book. To all of them I am deeply indebted, and I regret that they cannot all be recognized here. Several stand out because of the generous amount of time and wisdom they contributed when they appeared at Carnegie-Mellon University to lecture to my classes in crisis management held at the Graduate School of Industrial Administration in Pittsburgh, Pennsylvania.

At these sessions each described his or her approach to managing crises and related his or her personal experiences. I felt that none held anything back and that each made an indelible impression on the minds of our country's future business leaders. Consequently, everybody gained. Nowhere else had such a forum been convened, and no other students have benefited from such an experience. Further, the thoughts of these people reinforced my own convictions and added to my enthusiasm to produce this book. Those who provided me with this valuable assistance are:

William M. Agee	Former Chairman, Bendix Corporation
Warren M. Anderson	Chairman, Union Carbide Corporation
George A. Baker	Former Executive Vice President, Continental Illinois Corporation
Phillip J. Bakes	President, Continental Airlines
Philip Caldwell	Former Chairman, Ford Motor Company
David E. Collins	Vice Chairman, Johnson & Johnson
Kalman B. Druck	President, Kalman B. Druck, Inc.
George A. Ferris	Vice Chairman and CEO, Wheeling-Pittsburgh Steel Corporation
Douglas A. Fraser	Former President, United Auto Workers
Harry J. Gray	Chairman, United Technologies, Inc.
Pat Greathouse	Former Vice President, United Auto Workers
Karen N. Horn	President, Federal Reserve Bank of Cleveland
Richard J. Jacob	Chairman, Dayco Corporation
Donald D. Lennox	Chairman, Navistar International Corporation
Robert S. Leventhal	Chairman, Western Union Corporation
Archie McCardell	Former Chairman, International Harvester Corporation
Alonzo L. McDonald	Former President, Bendix Corporation
F. James McDonald	President, General Motors Corporation
Frank H. Menaker, Jr.	Vice President and General Counsel, Martin Marietta Corporation

Robert S. Miller, Jr.	Vice Chairman, Chrysler Corporation
T. Boone Pickens, Jr.	Chairman, Mesa Petroleum Corporation
Howard D. Putnam	Former Chairman, Braniff Airlines
Stuart M. Reed	President, Consolidated Rail Corporation
Frank J. Sellinger	Former Chairman, Schlitz Brewery
Ira Stepanian	President, Bank of Boston

Also deserving of special mention are those upon whom I leaned repeatedly for advice and counsel as I proceeded. I am grateful to Kalman B. Druck for the wealth of his knowledge and willingness to contribute his experience gained in decades of public perception crises and in countless other ways. He was always available, insightful, and encouraging.

I also want to thank Richard M. Cyert, president of Carnegie-Mellon University, and Elizabeth E. Bailey, dean of the Graduate School of Industrial Administration at CMU, for their confidence in my mission. They provided the platform and the free rein to pursue my subject and evidenced the enthusiasm necessary to move as fast as we did.

And I am indebted to all of my students who labored with me as I learned to be a professor. They ignored my warts because they, too, were excited to be pioneers on a new frontier of management. One student in particular, Patrick Langhoff, not only stayed the course but is responsible for much of the research that undergirds what you will read. He also served as a youthful conscience for this battle-scarred executive. I also want to thank Dr. Sidney Goldstein, head of cardiology at Detroit's Henry Ford Hospital, for sharing his knowledge in medical crisis management.

Finally, this whole effort would not have been possible

without the patient and wise counsel of my editor, William Strachan. He offered me a long leash and allowed me to run with my ideas until I was exhausted. Then he would deftly remind me of my limits and lead me back to a better and more scholarly trail. Every writer should have such fine artistic counsel. He and Raphael Sagalyn, my literary agent, gave me the early encouragement that brought this book into being.

Of course, I owe everything to my wife, Barbara, and children, Susan, Andy, and Nancy, who lived with me through the crises of writing about crisis. My family was my strength.

Contents

Three: Dealing with Disruption

Introduction

I awoke to hear a doctor whispering to my wife, "We want you to know he is in very serious trouble." The air smelled of alcohol and perspiration; the lights were blurry and I could hardly see. My entire body was draped with cold, wet towels. Even though I had regained consciousness, the doctor was preparing my wife for the possibility that I would not make it.

My problem was a common enough ailment — a kidney stone. Kidney stones don't kill people, I'd thought at first; they just hurt. But this one had induced a massive infection that sent my temperature spiking up to 106 degrees, and I was delirious for several days before the fever finally broke. The kidney stone had provoked an intense physical crisis. In an earlier era I probably would have died. The difference was modern medical care. The medical team, accustomed to dealing with events like mine, had coolly assessed the problem, sorted through the treatment options, and administered the needed care quickly and effectively.

As I was recovering, I had time to reflect on the subject

of crises. I had certainly seen enough of them in a thirty-odd-year career in the automobile business that had taken me from a management trainee to the chairmanship of the American Motors Corporation.

Most executives, I have found, do not like to think about crises. Those I have spoken with over the years avoid talking about the subject, even if it is clear that their companies have been through one. They equate a crisis with bad management; things like that just didn't happen on *their* watch.

But crises do happen, perhaps more frequently now than ever. From my hospital experience, I saw how the medical profession had developed ways of dealing with physical crises. Yet though there are similarities between medical and corporate crises, business surprisingly has not developed effective crisis management techniques. As I continued to think about dealing with crises and read the scant literature on the subject, Carnegie-Mellon University, my alma mater, suggested that I join the faculty to explore the matter on a scholarly basis.

Soon I had chief executives of major corporations appearing at weekly sessions before my graduate students to explain their particular crises and to defend their actions. These "live" accounts from the business battlefield by major participants added the strength of reality to our studies and the theories we were formulating.

I remember the session with William M. Agee especially well. He told the story of how his company, Bendix, had set out to acquire Martin Marietta and wound up merged out of existence. He was smooth and engaging, but he failed to sell the students on his argument that he had essentially won the battle with Martin Marietta's Thomas G. Pownall. Nevertheless, his account was instructive—in ways he probably did not intend—about the handling of a takeover crisis. What we learned from the discussions, as we shall see later, was that he was unprepared to go swimming with the sharks that populate the aerospace business. He was eaten alive.

Similarly, Frank J. Sellinger, the last chairman of Schlitz, told the chronicle of double-cross and intrigue that led to the smaller Stroh Brewery's taking control of his company. The message here was that Sellinger had accumulated too much cash without a clear plan of how to use it. We learned volumes from him, as we did from most of the chief executives who visited the classroom. And I came to realize that crisis management is a field as fertile as it is unploughed. Some public relations firms have recognized that top executives need techniques to manage crises, although their help is limited to crises involving public perception. Not all crises, however, fall within this area.

One organization that *has* attempted to come to grips with sudden crisis is the military. Command centers have been established at the Pentagon to absorb information and analyze it before advising senior administration officials at the White House whether to scramble jet bombers and open the hatches on the missile silos. This system, one of today's best-organized attempts to prepare for crisis management, was developed under the threat of a sudden nuclear war. But any account of it is couched in arcane terminology and is wrapped in the necessary cloak of security, making it largely unavailable to the outside world.

The hints we do have suggest that a lot of effort is given to imagining likely contingencies and our responses to them. I had some exposure to this process during the Korean War, as top secret control officer at Pepperill Air Force Base, near St. John's, Newfoundland. As the junior lieutenant on the base, I had nothing to do with the drafting of the emergency war plans I lugged from filing cabinet to filing cabinet, but I did get to see them. What I saw amazed me. Simulated wars were fought in great detail on paper. Bombing runs were planned down to the last pound of fuel needed by the aircraft and the last C ration for the crews. I came away with the distinct impression that, despite the time and effort lavished on them, the plans would have been useless unless an actual attack was exactly the same as the one anticipated. Though the military at least acknowledged that crises might occur, its projected reactions were an example of overplanning, not crisis management. Thank goodness we never had to rely on them.

Business is even more vulnerable to overplanning. We are now sixty years into the era of "scientific management" in business, a period during which we have sought to transform management from an art form to a discipline that can be mastered by study and the application of proven theories. But it seems that the scientific approach to business, with its stress on systematic planning and structured management, has obscured the need for finding ways of responding to change and impending crisis.

Perhaps we have been worshiping an imperfect god. In our emphasis on planning and tight financial controls, we have decided implicitly that a crisis happens only when our know-how fails. We have concluded that the correct response to trouble is better planning and tighter controls. But crisis is still very much with us. Maybe it is time to stop trying to plan our way out of problems and consider an alternative—managing them.

PART ONE

The Argument

1

Crisis Management

MOST ORGANIZATIONS are reluctant to prepare for adversity. Leaders in any field find failure distasteful. It is difficult for them to admit that they or the organizations they head have been guilty of poor performance. Every aggressive, successful person is conditioned to

- Think success
- Plan for success
- Allow no negative thinking
- Associate with positive people
- Emphasize accomplishment and cast off losers

Harold Geneen, the legendary boss of ITT, has made this attitude central to his management technique. His slogan is "Management must manage," and he urges his prospective followers to repeat it three times. He says this is "probably the closest thing to the secret of success in business . . . in everything you undertake." He maintains that once you have set a business objective, you *must* achieve it. Those who fail to do so, he says, are not simply poor managers; they are not managers at all.

This sort of mind-set ill prepares a business to deal with the reversals that can befall even the best-managed company. Although preparing for the worst circumstance is distasteful, the company that does not do so—does not prepare for the possibility that its plans may not work, that the assumptions and conditions that underlie the plans may change quickly—will too often find itself unable to deal with a crisis. It may suffer enormous material and personnel losses.

A large measure of the responsibility for urging reluctant managers to prepare for a darkening of their typically rosy outlook lies with the board of directors. But most boards are content with a passive role. All they know is what they learn from the CEO, who is not likely to advertise his mistakes. As a result, many a board doesn't know the roots of a crisis when it strikes, and, consequently, will be of little use in dealing with it. Lacking knowledge and a contingency program of their own, a board usually gets rid of top management. It fires the old team and installs another set of positive-thinking, strive-for-success managers without learning what the cause of the problem was. Too often the process is repetitious, with the new group destined to be swept away by the same forces that did in its predecessors.

This was true for a while at American Motors Corporation. AMC is a big company, with revenues of over $4 billion a year, but by the gargantuan standard of the American automobile industry, where General Motors alone has sales of over $90 billion a year, it was simply too small. It couldn't have the broad product line, the range of options, the conveniently located dealers, that its larger rivals already had in place. What AMC fundamentally needed was to be part of a larger organization that could supply the needed resources but that didn't stop it from trying to find some sort of magic from 1953, when Hudson and Nash merged to form AMC, until 1979, at which time we arranged a partnership with the French company Renault.

A succession of CEOs began with George Romney, who sold fuel-efficient cars twenty years before there was any real need for them. Roy Abernethy followed Romney and reversed his predecessor's course, shifting back to big cars. Abernethy fitted the cartoon image of a Detroit auto mogul. He chewed big black Corona-Corona cigars and waved the soggy end at subordinates. One of his quirks was to wear a hat to the styling studio so that he could make sure there was enough headroom in the new models. On one of his visits he plopped down in the back of a prototype and when his hat brushed the headliner, demanded that the roof be raised. That is why a 1960s' model called the Marlin is one of the few cars that ever had a roof sloping toward the front.

There were others, including Roy D. Chapin, Jr., and William V. Luneberg, but their efforts were limited by the structure of the industry. The company replaced managers after each crisis, but this did not deal with the underlying conditions nor adapt the company to fit them.

There is a larger theme here: business managers need to break out of the cycle of everyday planning and deal openly and directly with the subject of crisis. They need to accept a crisis for what it is—a warning that a turning point is near. Then they can take action. The circumstances that led to the crisis should be carefully studied so that the same mistakes won't be made again. And the opportunities created by a crisis should be sought out even as damage control is under way. A lot can be done during a crisis that would be difficult or impossible to accomplish during a business-as-usual period.

Business must develop a theory of crisis management that will be of practical use to managers.

My hope is that business can prepare to manage crises as skillfully as medicine does.

THE LESSONS OF MEDICINE

A battlefield is a scene of continuous crisis. From the time when our forebears used clubs to today's sophisticated weaponry, the objective of a battle has always been the same: to inflict enough damage on the other side to win. With the evolution of medical technology, those who treat the casualties of battle have come to rely on procedures that can provide useful models for business.

Wartime physicians have developed a crisis management system that allocates scarce resources so that they will do the most good. It is a brutal but effective system called triage. As the wounded are brought in for treatment, they are immediately classified into three groups:

1. The superficially wounded,
2. The hopelessly wounded,
3. The seriously wounded who have a chance for survival.

It is the last who get most of the attention, because they can benefit the most from medical care. Whatever resources remain are directed to the less seriously wounded, with the hopeless left to die in as much comfort as can be arranged. Heartless as it seems, the system maximizes the overall good by not wasting time and effort on the doomed.

Business has something to learn from this stern discipline and from the techniques that have been developed to manage illness with modern facilities and techniques. Obviously the tactics will be different, but the approach taken by doctors in assessing and dealing with physical emergencies bears close study.

Medicine has never had to overcome the attitudinal barrier of the positive thinkers. Rather than deny that critical events will happen, physicians have prepared to deal with them in a routine but thoughtful way.

Consider, for example, what would happen if you were in a traffic accident on the way to work. The first response of helpful passersby is to call for an emergency medical truck. If you are fortunate enough to live in an area where there is up-to-date equipment, a vehicle will soon arrive staffed by technicians and equipped with a full range of medical supplies and the means of communicating with a nearby hospital.

Paramedics on the ambulance can transmit your vital signs to doctors at the hospital so that they can evaluate your condition and devise a plan of treatment while you are in transit. At the emergency room door, you are met by a crew of medical people who already know a lot about you and are ready to administer tests and begin treatment.

If your injuries are really serious, you will probably be moved to another of medicine's crisis response centers, the intensive care unit. There, hooked up to monitoring equipment that can detect signs of incipient trouble, you will be the focus of the best and most concentrated care that medical professionals can provide. Once the immediate crisis has passed, you will probably be shifted to another section of the hospital for whatever additional treatment you need.

At each level, the medical response corresponds to the gravity of your problem. At each level the professionals' purpose is similar: to gain as much information as quickly as possible and then to begin treatment. Although economics are not explicitly mentioned, the need to keep costs under control has a major influence on medical decisions; you are not going to be in that intensive care unit a day more than is necessary.

ACCEPTING A CRISIS

It is no condemnation of a person's business acumen when his plan starts going wrong—so wrong that the life of a company is threatened—nor is crisis something that always befalls the other guy. Usually there was nothing particularly bad about the plan or even the assumptions it was built on. What most often happens is that the assumptions have quietly eroded, undetected, undermining the most carefully crafted plan like sand that's been washed from beneath a sea wall.

Once crisis has been accepted as a normal—if less than pleasant—circumstance, the next step is to find commercial counterparts to the emergency treatments devised by medicine.

In trying to understand how crises affect business organizations, I found it useful to consider psychiatrist Elisabeth Kübler-Ross's studies of the terminally ill. She discovered that most patients, once they become aware that they are suffering from a fatal affliction, generally pass through five stages in coming to grips with their impending death:

1. Denial and isolation
2. Anger
3. Bargaining for time
4. Depression and grief
5. Acceptance

I believe this model is a good starting point for understanding the pathology of crisis in business. Many times the same progression of attitudes occurs within a business organization when the people inside it begin to recognize the fatal symptoms.

Even closer to the point is the work done by Stephen L. Fink, Joel Bean, and Kenneth Taddeo and discussed in their article "Organizational Crisis and Change" in the *Journal of Applied Behavioral Science* (1971, 7 [1]). They found that companies go through four distinct stages when struck by unexpected trouble:

1. Shock
2. Defensive retreat
3. Acknowledgment
4. Adaptation and change

Having moved from the personal and medical analogies to the business environment, we have a better foundation to assess the management of a crisis, as well as to identify the nature of business crises.

The Types of Crises

There are today nine distinct types of business crises. Each has its own symptoms and treatment, and though each is different from the others, all have some common characteristics. The nine crises are:

1. Public perception
2. Sudden market shift
3. Product failure
4. Top management succession
5. Cash
6. Industrial relations
7. Hostile takeover
8. Adverse international events
9. Regulation and deregulation

We all think we know about public perception crises because our newspapers and television tell us about them all the time. And that is a big part of the problem: I can't think of a single case in which I was personally involved that the media got the story absolutely straight. The natural tendency of many companies to clam up when things go wrong doesn't make the press's job any easier, but ask any insider at Union Carbide or E. F. Hutton whether the real story of what happened at Bhopal or with the bank overdrafts has been told. Corporate misdeeds as well as an imperfect system of reporting contribute to these crises.

The sudden market shift is usually no secret to the general public either. Indeed, the public is usually responsible for it. Consider the abrupt rise and fall of video games and the corresponding impact on Warner's Atari division. Even in industries that live on changing tastes, such as women's fashions, a sharp reaction by the public can find a manufacturer tooled up to make midiskirts when the retailers can't give them away.

Mention the Dalkon Shield or Rely tampons, and most women wince. Both are products that failed—and with good reason; they were serious threats to the health of their users. Early and strong crisis management can minimize the effects of such failures, and the lack of it can make a bad situation worse.

Frequently top managers refuse to give way to successors, touching off a crisis of top management succession. Dr. Armand Hammer has relieved several aspirants before they could become a real threat to his apparent lifetime control of Occidental Petroleum. Harry J. Gray at United Technologies was similarly reluctant to depart. When Lew Glucksman shoved Pete Peterson out of the top job at Lehman Brothers, the firm did not survive the crisis. Succession is one area where the board of directors has complete control and can act to prevent a crisis before it develops.

The Chrysler Corporation and Lee Iacocca epitomize all that can be said about managing a cash shortage crisis during a recession. Every business school warns about the danger of cash shortage crises; few tell their students what to do about them.

In 1979, International Harvester got involved in a bitter strike that nearly killed it. That such a historic company was able to survive only in much reduced form is testimony to the destructive power of the industrial relations crisis. Even though organized labor's power is shrinking in America, the consequence of a miscalculation in treating people—organized or not—can be enormous.

An unfriendly attack from the outside is a serious threat to a publicly owned company at any time, particularly in this era of "junk bonds." Martin Marietta was prepared when Bill Agee attacked in 1982; that's why it prevailed.

Caterpillar, long regarded as one of the best-managed companies in the country, has suffered from adverse international events, notably the strength of the dollar against other currencies. This makes Cat's big machines more expensive than those coming from Japan, and has cost the company dearly in export markets.

Finally, there is the problem of regulation and deregulation. For years the government went one way, piling regulation after regulation on industry, regardless of the costs. Then the political winds shifted, and the process reversed itself. Dealing with an unregulated market, with lots of start-up competition and high costs baked in, can be a bracing experience, as some major airlines have found. Harding Lawrence of Braniff misjudged what would happen once the Civil Aeronautics Board was abolished, and the company collapsed from overexpansion. In many ways, sudden deregulation is more of a problem than slow, predictable regulation.

Each crisis that erupts seems to be unique and strange. Yet if we examine the origins and the sequence of events, we can find many common elements. This pattern of predictability is the key to forecasting business crises and for moderating their effects. The ability to foretell events is exciting—and I think we are getting close to just that.

2

The Unmanaged Crisis

AN UNMANAGED CRISIS is a horror. It makes no difference whether it is in business, the military, or medicine. It strikes, apparently without warning, and there is no knowing the outcome. All you are sure of is that you are in the middle of a crisis and it is scaring you to death.

There is the distinct possibility that the very terror of the situation will push you into taking actions that will make things even worse. When William Brown, the chairman of the Bank of Boston, realized that the public was to learn of the bank's unreported transfer from abroad of $1.2 billion in cash, he reacted first with silence and then with statements that only drew more attention to the bank's misdeeds. He tried vainly to minimize the affair, claiming that no individual fault could be found. Moreover, he claimed there was "no evidence whatsoever" that anybody at the bank had "benefitted in any way."

The bank's top managers seemed to be thoroughly frightened by the disclosures, and the crisis raced ahead essentially unmanaged. Each attempt to lay the matter to rest with self-serving statements worked to the bank's detriment. Then the lending institution, two hundred years old, the largest and strongest in New England, admitted that it was guilty of laundering funds from questionable sources and was fined the maximum $500,000. After the scandal broke, the bank admitted to having been informed of its improper reporting of cash transfers and its strange behavior in shielding the transactions of a family that has since been convicted of organized crime. The actions themselves were bad enough; the mismanagement of the crisis once it was in the open only made things worse.

THE STAGES OF CRISIS

Precrisis Period

Unmanaged crises, regardless of their individual circumstances, follow a pattern. Once we understand the dynamics of a crisis, we can choose the tools to help us shape its outcome.

First we must recognize a crisis's onset, which is not as difficult as it may seem. Usually there is a definite *precrisis* period, something like the aura before a migraine headache: you know something is wrong, but just what is not clear. This period is marked by three distinct stages.

The first stage is simple *nonperformance:* someone or some group is not getting the job done. The initial failure is small, but then it happens again and again. These repeated bungles, though not of any great magnitude, are a tip-off. Sales quotas not met, cash flows that do not meet projections, production schedules missed, quality targets unachieved, budgets busted, receivables aging badly, prototypes developing flaws, advertising missing the market, excessive turnover of people, or inventories out of line are all examples of nonperformance. At this stage, the problems are usually overlooked by top management.

It is when the problems are recognized that the second stage begins; this is usually a prolonged period of *denial*. "It isn't true," says the boss. "If we just have a little perspective," he continues, "and take some time to put things into context, we'll see that the problems are not really serious and will probably go away."

When they do not go away, and the errors begin to mount, the company slips toward the third and final stage of the precrisis period. The dominant emotions now are *anger* and *fear*. Finger pointing begins; rivalries flare. When Schlitz changed its beer formula and started losing market share (which was not spotted at the time because of a strike at the industry leader, Anheuser-Busch), the entire precrisis period was a classic sequence of repeated failures in the marketplace, rapid changes in management, and a welling-up of recrimination and anger at all levels. Before the company could be stabilized, it had been taken over by a smaller competitor.

The precrisis period is just the beginning, however, and is usually not visible to the outside world. Management is worried and torn internally, but the public is not permitted to know, and is usually not really interested in learning, what is going on behind the corporate door. That makes it a time of opportunity for the company. If the senior management or the directors are alert enough to recognize the danger, they can do a great deal to keep the damage from becoming a full-blown crisis.

In fact, one of the greatest responsibilities of top management is to detect early evidence of the repeated sequence of nonperformance, denial and recrimination, and anger and fear. In order to do so, management must be in touch with operations at all levels. "Management by walking around" is what Thomas Peters and Robert Waterman labeled it in *In Search of Excellence*. Any good executive knows that one of the harshest penalties of isolation from the troops and a lack of direct involvement is the danger of being overcome by the unexpected—but few recognize that this precrisis period exists and that awareness of it can be enormously valuable in allowing management to take deterrent action. It may be late, but getting involved early is better than waiting until all hell breaks loose.

The Crisis Period

For those who have not acted in time, the world caves in. No longer is there just a gradual buildup of difficulty and resentment; no longer is the public unaware. Management can't hide the problems from itself or anyone else. The next phase of the uncontrolled crisis is the crisis period itself—and it is awful.

All crises cause pain. The pain may be expressed in dollars lost, career opportunities destroyed, or the sheer emotional burden borne by executives trying to cope with its effects. It is all of these and more. Like the concept of utility in economics, it cannot be measured precisely (at least not at this time), but, like utility, it can be ordered. You can't tell your doctor that your pain ranks 7.5 on the Richter scale, but you sure know when the hurt gets better or worse.

The pain produced by a crisis follows a predictable path over time. In the precrisis phase, it increases slowly. When the actual crisis strikes, the pain shoots upward like an angry fever until it climaxes. As the crisis passes, it slowly declines, but it ends at a level higher than it was before the episode began.

When a crisis strikes, there is no time for recriminations;

Pain Curve

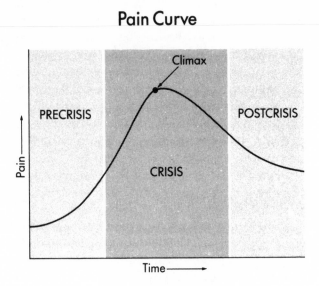

it is too late to take preventive measures. All a chief executive can do now is react, try to minimize the damage, buy time, and prepare for better days.

The first stage in the crisis period is *failure*—failure of devastating proportions and visible for all to see.

Reactions to Crisis

All the people involved with a company are affected, many of them deeply. Customers are shocked. If the company produces a consumer product, and the product itself is under attack, sales can come to a stunning halt. The little Chevrolet Corvair, an innovative piece of engineering, suffered a death blow when Ralph Nader published *Unsafe at Any Speed*.

Employees at every level of the company are stunned and lose a sense of common purpose and cohesiveness.

Top managers feel the pressure in social situations. The bad jokes on the subject hurt; the overheard remarks and comments in the newspapers can take a toll on a manager's attitude toward himself and his company.

The worst reactions usually are those of creditors and lending institutions. They want to know why they weren't informed about the problems sooner—a good question, but not a particularly useful one once the crisis is at hand. Management is looking for help at this point, not Monday morning quarterbacking. But lenders have to be satisfied if the financial structure of the company depends on their support, as it usually does.

I recall a period at AMC in the early 1980s when we were hit by the second recession during the Reagan administration. It has been described as the worst economic setback for the country since the Great Depression, and it was completely unexpected. Car and truck sales plummeted overnight from ten million a year to six million. Trucks, which included our Jeeps, were the worst off.

Our new lead bank, which we had chosen after deciding to end a long association with Chase Manhattan, had no experience with the automobile business. When the market died in just ninety days, the bank's top lending officer was horrified. He was so upset that when we neared a small technical default on our credit agreement, he wanted to call the entire loan, which would have been sure death for AMC. Fortunately, we were able to calm things down. Lending institutions have a low threshold of pain when conditions are uncertain.

Others are drawn into the crisis. Your suppliers are sympathetic to a point, because they want to keep your business. They profess loyalty, but if you look hard, you can see they are preparing for your decline or demise.

Probably the groups that managers find hardest to deal with as the crisis hits are the government and regulatory agencies. A failure that in any way affects the public usually brings about increased scrutiny by the government and an added burden of regulation. The last thing a company needs when the ground is shaking is the government's asking to get involved. As somebody said long ago, the three common statements most likely to be false are "Your check is in the mail," "I gave at the office," and "I'm from the government and I'm here to help."

After the failure, *panic* starts to set in. Events are unstructured; people are running on adrenaline; personal survival becomes paramount. Solutions are hard to define because the problems are not always completely obvious. Getting good information about what is happening is difficult because much of what is being reported is colored by emotion. Whatever good data are available are subject to differing interpretations. Values clash. Management differences that formerly were set aside or quashed by everyone's concerted effort to achieve clear-cut goals—or to thwart a common enemy—begin to emerge, and infighting begins. The goals now become fuzzy, conflicting, dispersed.

Whatever constraints that hampered the company before—lack of capital, management deficiencies, powerful competitors, stiff regulations—become enormous obstacles. Management always has to ration time and resources, but when panic strikes, the limitations seem even more stringent. Furthermore, the organization is often weakened by a breakdown of respect among the lower ranks for top managers. The role models have been shown to have clay feet, and those who deferred to greater accomplishment and experience feel ill served. Things formerly taken for granted are challenged. Decisions are debated rather than obeyed. The organization becomes fluid and shapeless.

Dealing with Ambiguity

At this point the most helpful of the survivors are those managers who can handle conflict, accept ambiguity, and deal with paradox. Not many executives are comfortable with these tasks or do them well. One of the critical problems for a company in the midst of a crisis is brain drain as the best managers seek safety elsewhere. Of those who remain, many are so distracted by the uncertainties that they are not effective.

The rare executives who are best at dealing with crises are those who have a high tolerance for the unstructured and can hold several conflicting views simultaneously until a resolution is found. These people can accept ambiguity because they understand that by denying it, they may reject an eventual solution or too hastily accept a conclusion without having enough information. Indeed, as Michael B. McCaskey wrote in *The Executive Challenge: Managing Change and Ambiguity,* people like this regard a period of uncertainty as a rewarding and rich experience. Rewarding because it offers opportunities for personal and corporate advancement; rich because it provides intellectual stimulation.

There are others in whom, according to McCaskey, "the experience of ambiguity arouses anxiety and the need for more control. To tolerate ambiguity seems to imply some sort of personal failure of understanding or skill." An executive with a firstrate brain seeks situations that pose challenge and there are few greater challenges in business than those that occur during the failure period of a crisis.

The End Approaches

If, however, the people and systems are not up to the challenge and the crisis period continues unmanaged, the company is headed for *collapse*. The organization, the people, the public, lenders, suppliers, and, of course, the customers begin to give up. The attempt to keep the ship afloat ceases; it begins to sink.

Chrysler Corporation encountered this peril several times, most recently in the late 1970s, when it became clear that the company was not prepared to move into the next decade with the people and products it had on hand. Burdened with a huge cost structure and unable to raise funds, it could not make the investments needed to meet the onslaught from the Orient. Everyone in the auto industry knew that John Riccardo, then CEO, was doing everything humanly possible under the old system to make it work, but that it was just not enough. Chrysler was beset by government regulation, competitive pressures, and its own ineptness. The disarray was obvious. Panic started to set in, and collapse was imminent. It was only when the system was changed, when Lee Iacocca and his new team of managers—fortified with federal guarantees for $1.2 billion in loans—took charge that the company was able to continue until the national economy improved. Iacocca's new management techniques pared the company back to its core car and light-truck business, broke the cycle of the unmanaged crisis, and kept Chrysler from going under.

Postcrisis Period

The last phase of an unmanaged crisis is characterized by *shock* and *uncertainty*. People are immobilized. Hope is lost, and only the hardiest—or the foolhardy—stay around to pick over the bones. The banks have long ago shifted the company to the "work-out" department, which is supposed to find a way of getting back at least some of its money. Usually, though, the work-out people don't know quite what to do, since calling the debt will result in only more losses.

Among the most concerned and potentially the most effective group is the board of directors. In itself, it can act as a crisis management team that takes hold of the company—preferably with the chief executive, but without him if necessary—and searches for alternatives to oblivion for the shareholders and everyone else involved. Unfortunately, by the time matters have reached this point, the board is as preoccupied with protecting itself as with saving the wealth of the shareholders.

If nothing effective has been done to this point, the unmanaged crisis is at the final stage, *radical change*. If the company is fortunate, it will have a core business that may be attractive to a new investor. More often, the end will bring about a restructuring under Chapter 11 of the federal bankruptcy laws so that a new and lesser entity can be formed. If neither of these options is available, there looms the specter of liquidation or absorption by another company.

This, then, is the form of an unmanaged crisis:

Stage	*Sequence*
Precrisis:	Nonperformance $\longrightarrow$ Denial/Recrimination $\longrightarrow$ Anger/Fear
Crisis:	Failure $\longrightarrow$ Panic $\longrightarrow$ Collapse
Postcrisis:	Shock $\longrightarrow$ Uncertainty $\longrightarrow$ Radical change

Crises rarely occur in their purest form. Most proceed slowly during their early phases, unnoticed by top management and the board until failure comes crashing down. Sometimes somebody tries to take hold at this point and may succeed in delaying the collapse and radical change. Some, such as Lee Iacocca at Chrysler, can actually reverse the sickening slide and restore a company's health. What results, though, will usually look a lot different from the company that underwent the crisis in the first place.

Unless a crisis is managed, the sequence of its stages is fairly predictable. It is during the precrisis period that detection and intervention will do the most good.

The second phase—the obvious failure, the attendant publicity, and the panic and collapse—is not a time for managers and strategic thinkers. It is a time for leadership and heroic efforts well beyond the daily efforts of even the best business executives.

In the postcrisis phase radical change will revise everything; control will pass to new players. The essential point of crisis management is to break the sequence of the unmanaged crisis and to redirect events. Later I will restructure this pattern into a program for successful crisis management and show how the sequence of events can be changed. Proper preparation can prevent some crises and minimize the impact of those which cannot be avoided.

The downside of a crisis, happily, is not the only side. A crisis can shake up the established order and make rapid changes possible. It can bring unusual opportunities as well as great dangers.

The Continental Illinois Bank

The failure of the Continental Illinois Bank in 1984 is a good example of what happens to a company when a crisis is mismanaged; each of the classic stages of crisis and its consequences were sharply visible. To be sure, many bankers were charting their way through the unfamiliar waters of deregulation and petrodollar recycling in the late 1970s, but Continental stands out because of its size and the magnitude of its misfortune.

The seeds of the crisis were sown in 1976, when the

chairman, Roger Anderson, decided to push for aggressive growth. At that time Continental was known as a reasonably successful midwestern lender, but Anderson decreed that it should become one of the nation's top three banks within ten years. The problem was that the bank was not prepared to grow rapidly. Its systems were dependent on personal contact between managers who had known each other for years. When the push for aggressive growth began, the safeguards in the old systems were inadequate. It was the nonperformance during this period that resulted in the later crisis.

At first all went well; Continental grew rapidly, with assets doubling to $47 billion by 1981. But there were some troubling signs: oil prices were softening and consumption was not growing; recession gripped the Midwest, undercutting the value of real estate. More ominously, Penn Square Bank, a storefront operation that had sold close to $1 billion in oil and gas credits to Continental, was under investigation by banking authorities. But when one bank officer wrote a memo suggesting caution in dealing with Penn Square, top managers denied that anything was amiss.

In July 1982 Penn Square failed, imposing heavy losses on Continental. Since Continental lacked a large retail banking base to supply it with funds, it had borrowed heavily from large domestic and foreign investors to fund its loan portfolio. As the worry about the bank's solvency rose, the price it had to pay for funds went up as well, increasing the financial pinch. Managers began departing and assets shrunk.

By the spring of 1984 Anderson was out as chief executive, and nonperforming loans totaled $2.3 billion. It was becoming harder for the bank to sell its certificates of deposit at any price, and rumors of insolvency were rife. In a desperate move to keep foreign banks from withdrawing

The Unmanaged Crisis of
The Continental Illinois Bank
(1976–1986)

PRECRISIS	CRISIS	POSTCRISIS
Nonperformance	*Failure*	*Shock*
Chairman Anderson sets new goal to be one of top 3 banks in U.S.	Rumors circulate	Assets plummet
Aggressive domestic lending	Foreign banks withdraw lines of credit	All confidence, credibility, and respect lost
Concentration on energy and speculative real estate	David Taylor replaces Anderson as CEO	Stock price plunges from $36.50 in '82 to $4.50 in '84
Bank grows 50% faster than others	Nonperforming loans reach $2.3B	
Loan officers given wide latitude	Rumors of merger with Japanese	
Bank reaches goal and is acclaimed top lender	Large investors withdraw funds	
Oil prices drop, energy prices sour		
Profits drop		
Denial/Recrimination	*Panic*	*Uncertainty*
Banking authorities investigate Penn Square	Bank cannot find funds	FDIC looks for merger partners
Penn Square audit qualified	Bank sells credit card business (to pay dividends)	No buyers will assume risk
VP Kathleen Kenefick memo questions Penn Square	Taylor telexes foreign banks asking them to "hold firm"	Runs cannot be stopped

Denial/Recrimination (cont'd)

Bank Executive VP, George Baker, says Penn Square not a concern
Penn Square fails
Bank officers discharged, retired, transferred (10 vps, 2 sr. vps, 1 exec. vp)
Heavy writeoffs — $220M

Panic (cont'd)

Dividends suspended

Anger/Fear

S/H class action suit, bunker mentality
Funds become more expensive for bank
International banks losing confidence
Loan customers do not recover from recession
Downward spiral continues
Officer compensation reduced
Good managers depart

Collapse

Bank borrows $3.6B from Fed
16 banks raise $4.5B to assist
$7.5B rescue to stop capital loss by FDIC
$46M withdrawal by Chicago Board of Trade
$10B run in one month alone
Feds cannot find interested buyer of bank

Radical Change

FDIC buys $3.5B of bad loans, injects $1B into bank, assumes control of 80% of stock
FDIC takes over
Taylor resigns
Swearingen (from Standard of Indiana) becomes CEO
FDIC replaces 10 directors

their funds altogether, Continental sent out a telex message urging them to "hold firm."

The message had the opposite effect; foreign banks pulled out as quickly as they could, leaving Continental stricken. It borrowed from the Federal Reserve Board in an effort to maintain solvency and accepted a $4.5 billion aid package from sixteen other banks. The Federal Deposit Insurance Corporation worked up a $7.5 billion rescue plan, but was unable to find another bank willing to take over what was left of Continental.

Assets plunged from a high of $47 billion to $31 billion in less than three years. The price of the bank's stock dropped from $36.50 a share in 1982 to $4.50 a share in 1984. Nobody wanted Continental, but its complete failure would have sent tremors through the tightly linked financial system. Finally, the FDIC arranged a bailout, buying $3.4 billion of Continental's loans and injecting another $1 billion of capital. In return, the federal agency assumed control of 80 percent of the bank's stock, replaced top management, and replaced most of the board of directors. Nonperformance and then denial had led to a crisis, and radical change was the ultimate result.

The events at Continental illustrate clearly an unmanaged business crisis; each of the steps of mismanagement is unmistakable, and we can see how damaging it is to delay crisis intervention. At any stage of this cycle, it would have been better to break the cycle than let it spin on to its awful end. Instead the crisis engulfed and then all but destroyed one of the more important banks in the Midwest.

In itself the failure of Continental makes the case for better crisis management in business. As a case study of crisis management, it vividly lays out the pathology of a disease.

3

The Benefits of Crisis

WHEN WE THINK of crisis, we think of trouble. A comfortable routine has been broken; decisions have to be made on the basis of inadequate information and under enormous pressure. Who knows how it will all work out?

It is a mistake to think of crises only in negative terms. There is usually a positive side to critical events, one that should be recognized and used. Crises present opportunities as well as challenges, opportunities that are not available at any other time.

The reason they permit a degree of change unmatched in ordinary times is that all the old rules have been set aside. The crisis of war pulls fractious nations together to fend off an attacker, as was seen in World War II. The economic slump of the early 1980s, and the resulting layoffs, prompted formerly militant unions to accept contract concessions they would have vetoed earlier. The important thing is to recognize these rare moments of opportunity and seize them.

THE POTENTIAL ADVANTAGES OF CRISIS

There are seven gains that may accompany or result from a business crisis:

1. Heroes are born.
2. Change is accelerated.
3. Latent problems are faced.
4. People can be changed.
5. New strategies evolve.
6. Early warning systems develop.
7. New competitive edges appear.

We will examine thirty-one recent cases of real business crises. Some were poorly managed and the results predictably bad; in other instances, staggering wrecks were turned into vibrant corporations. Some present obvious lessons to be learned; others are merely experiences to be remembered. But what these cases make clear is that most crises provide opportunities of one sort or another. Seize them even while you are still trying to control the damage. In fact, there are some situations where it is necessary to provoke a crisis before any real progress can be made. Remember that the opportunities of a crisis can make the whole wrenching process endurable.

The Birth of Heroes

New leaders emerge from the smoke and din of crisis. It is true on the battlefield and is equally so in commerce. Even though Lee Iacocca had been a hotshot at Ford before going to Chrysler, his reputation was limited to Detroit and the auto industry. He was certainly not the national folk hero he has since become. He took on the challenge at Chrysler after he had been fired by Henry

Ford II. He threw himself into his new task even after finding that the situation was worse than he had imagined. He changed the company's strategy, got the government-backed loans, squeezed concessions out of everyone, and pulled the company back from the abyss. He became the image of the scrappy American battling decay in the Rust Belt. The value of his performance in selling Chrysler's cars has been incalculable; one dealer said customers were coming into his showroom looking for "four-door Iacoccas."

His success has reflected on others. Three of his closest associates were virtually unknown before the crisis at Chrysler, yet today they are recognized among the sharpest people in the auto industry. Gerald Greenwald was buried down in South America, running Ford's operations in Venezuela. Today he is a member of the five-man committee that runs Chrysler, is chairman of its Chrysler Motors subsidiary, and is generally acknowledged as Iacocca's heir. Robert S. (Steve) Miller was Greenwald's financial man in Venezuela. Today he is also a member of the corporate executive committee at Chrysler and chairman of the rapidly growing company's financial operations. Harold Sperlich was fired from Ford before Iacocca was, and he went to Chrysler as an assistant to a vice president. Now he is the president of Chrysler Motors and is hailed as one of the most talented product development and operations people in the industry. It took a crisis like the one at Chrysler to bring these men to the fore. Without it, they would be indistinguishable from the blur of thousands of auto executives who work in obscurity every day. They are not quite the national heroes, like Iacocca, but they are certainly prominent in their industry and have been amply rewarded for their efforts.

Sanford Sigoloff started out as just another struggling junior executive and was not particularly well known before he was asked to take over the faltering Wickes group of retail stores. But by the time he had led the company into and back out of Chapter 11, sold the unprofitable outlets, and rejuvenated the likely winners, he had a company so healthy that he had to spend $1 billion to buy out Gulf & Western's industrial businesses just to keep raiders away from his door. In his own way, Sigoloff is as successful as Iacocca and as much a hero. It was the crisis at Wickes that put him in control and allowed his talents to flourish.

Donald D. Lennox at International Harvester—now Navistar International—joined the truck and farm implement company in 1979, with Archie R. McCardell. But an industrial relations crisis, caused by a bitter six-month strike in 1979–1980, was followed by a steep slump in sales, and the IHC board ousted McCardell as CEO and tapped Lennox for the position. He has risen to the occasion, despite a background seemingly unsuited to the job, and pulled the company back to profitability by selling all operations except heavy trucks. Some still doubt that Navistar will remain a strong presence in its market because of the fierce competition it faces and its high labor costs, but Lennox has succeeded in keeping the company afloat through its most difficult period since its founding, in the mid-nineteenth century.

Frank Lorenzo and Phillip J. Bakes at Continental Airlines also distinguished themselves as business heroes born out of crisis. Taking the company into Chapter 11 to repudiate noncompetitive labor contracts did not make them very popular with the unions, but it did push the airline to a good level of profitability. More important, it assured Continental's future in the era of proliferating low-cost, low-fare carriers that followed deregulation.

The examples are many. The message is that crises can create leaders. Talented people who get the opportunity break the bonds of bureaucracy and show what they can accomplish. Even for a middle- or lower-level manager, a crisis is the big chance to take on hazardous but potentially rewarding assignments, work with new people, learn to live with ambiguity, and score big points. A crisis changes the established order, allowing talent to rise to the top.

Accelerated Change

Crisis compresses time. What previously had been unfolding slowly begins to quicken as chaos threatens; a crisis can cut years from the normal pace of progress. Those who seek change should welcome crisis. Although there are undesirable side effects to most crises that are also accelerated, they are a small price to pay for progress.

Union Carbide was shaken to its organizational core by the world's worst industrial accident, the one at Bhopal. Until that time, UC was a large but relatively undistinguished member of the nation's basic chemical industry, riding up and down with the industry's swings. The company's management was gradually moving it away from its dependence on commodity chemicals and was slowly reorganizing and reorienting its operations.

After the initial shock of the tragedy passed, the company became aware of its enormous vulnerability. If even a small fraction of the lawsuits filed on behalf of the victims resulted in judgments, the financial damage would be staggering. And it was also laid open to outside attack. Subsequently, GAF, a much smaller chemical company, launched a massive takeover effort (that eventually failed).

But faced with the threat from the outside in addition to the Bhopal crisis, UC got moving. It undertook a $1.06 billion restructuring of its major activities; dismissal notices went to fourteen hundred salaried employees in nine months; nonperforming assets were sold and written off; and plans were announced to buy back a major block of common stock. The Bhopal crisis quickened the pace of change at Carbide; new tactics became urgent and meaningful.

For several years, Schlitz beer had been slowly making its way into the market for lighter and sweeter beers. It had also changed its basic beer formula several times in the late 1960s and early 1970s to drive down costs. Then the crisis struck. The public decided that they were being cheated out of the product they had come to expect. Competitors made things worse by broadcasting the change. That gave Stroh's, a much smaller, family-held company, the chance it needed to launch an attack that hastened Schlitz's demise by years.

Facing Problems

It is human nature to avoid confronting one's most serious problems by a flurry of everyday activity. On rare occasions this turns out to be smart; sometimes troubles do go away, or the passage of time changes circumstances and reduces the difficulty. Most of the time, though, delay just makes things worse. To modify the old saying, "If it's broke, fix it quickly." If not, a crisis will force the repair.

Richard J. Jacob, the CEO at Dayco, had a first-class crisis in public perception. He had always considered the press to be hostile and was so inwardly oriented that he did not know how to react when *The Wall Street Journal* revealed that he had accepted phony orders from Russia to keep his factories running. Suddenly he had to face the press, which he saw as an adversary, while being accused of possible corruption. At the same time, he had to tighten the loose controls over foreign transactions that had allowed the whole mess to develop. The crisis forced him to learn how to deal with outsiders and at the same time make his internal operations more disciplined. He probably would have done neither had there not been a crisis.

A. H. Robins had problems with its Dalkon Shield, an intrauterine contraceptive device, from the outset. The evidence of injury and death was ignored at first and then denied. The company faced up to its product problems very late in the game—too late to save it from bankruptcy and loss of reputation. The crisis brought to light not only a serious product liability problem, but also a management style that could not confront such difficulties. Because of the crisis, subsequent managers are not likely to let anything like the Dalkon Shield incident happen again.

Procter & Gamble, on the other hand, reacted quickly and properly in withdrawing its Rely tampons when they became associated with toxic shock syndrome. Because it responded effectively, P & G's crisis passed quickly, and the company did not incur the damage suffered by Robins.

Moving People

In ordinary times it is difficult to make major changes in a company's labor force and management ranks without provoking anxiety, resentment, and union opposition. Lawyers are eager to file discrimination suits of all sorts on behalf of dismissed or even transferred employees. The maze of laws and regulations that guard an employee's "right" to a job are so complex that it is hard to decide in advance which ones will be upheld. A crisis, however, is a good environment for change.

E. F. Hutton is one of the oldest and best-known names in the stock brokerage business. It had grown up as a loose confederation of regional offices with little central control from headquarters in New York. When Hutton pleaded guilty to thousands of charges of illegally overdrafting bank accounts, there were changes in the way the company was managed and a lot of different faces on the scene. Robert Fomon is still chairman but has lost much of his power; a new president, Robert P. Rittereiser, has been brought in from Merrill Lynch, and the former chief financial officer and legal counsel have gone. These changes would not have happened—in fact, would have been thought unnecessary—had there not been a crisis, but analysts think Hutton will become stronger because of them.

There are always exceptions to a rule, and on the surface United Technologies appears to be one. The management succession crisis that afflicted that organization for so many years has still not brought about the complete unseating of Harry Gray. But it has had an important effect: Gray was finally forced to name a successor. It may be some years before the younger man really grasps the reins of power, but at least an end to Gray's dominance can be envisioned. The ouster of Gray's four previous potential successors finally forced the UT board to make Gray agree that his days are not infinite.

The succession problems at Lehman Brothers were hidden by the façade of Wall Street wealth and success. Then came the explosion. Lewis Glucksman forced out Peter Peterson, and there followed a rebellion in the ranks that crumbled the venerable firm and sent Glucksman into well-padded retirement. Pete Peterson and Lew Glucksman had been in a power struggle for years. Some of the partners thought they could restore stability by accepting Peterson's resignation and turning over power to Glucksman, but the situation became so unstable that the company slipped into the clutches of American Express.

The management slate was wiped clean twice at Braniff Airlines. First, Harding Lawrence was ousted for his ill-advised rush to overexpand following deregulation; then the succeeding team of Howard D. Putnam and Philip M. Guthrie failed to avert bankruptcy. Crisis can force personnel changes when management tries to find answers.

New Strategies

There is nothing inherently wrong with planning. Planning is routine, but following plans is one of the most mindless activities of management. The real challenge lies in changing the plan—or planning for change. The greatest obstacles to change are inertia and habit. Changing a strategic plan requires almost an act of God in the board room, even if the basis for the existing plan has changed. There is great comfort in having made up one's mind about a difficult issue and then simply carrying out what has been decided.

A crisis forces reconsideration of even the most cherished plans. The threat to a business's prosperity, the uncertainty, the pressure, and the lack of control all permit new thoughts to come to the surface and new directions to be considered. It is at these times that new strategies evolve.

Perhaps one of the best examples of a new business strategy emerging from a crisis is that of General Motors. The two oil crises of the 1970s loosened GM's headlock on the American auto marketplace. Since then, top management has been turning the gigantic corporation inside out, reorganizing it to cope with the threat of the imports. The company has also changed its basic strategy.

GM's approach in the past was to be integrated as vertically as possible in its manufacturing and to have a product line-up that would entice buyers to purchase larger and more expensive cars as they advanced in age and economic standing. But the oil crises doomed the really large cars, and the formidable efficiency of the Japanese have made domestic small-car production uneconomic. So GM has changed, putting a Chevrolet "bow tie" logo on small cars made in Japan. Soon GM will be selling cars made in Korea, and it is shopping the world over for low-cost components. Ten years ago, all this would have been unthinkable, and it is unlikely that GM would have moved as fast as it has without the spur of crisis.

The crisis at Caterpillar Tractor also caused a shift in strategy. Confronting a continuing depression in the sales of farm and construction equipment, it abandoned its long-term strategy of premium pricing and turned to discounting to grab as much market share as it could. It also abandoned its "made in the U.S.A." stance and set up factories overseas to take advantage of lower costs. And, facing an extended battle in the marketplace with both domestic and foreign competition, it is undergoing an extended period of corporate contraction.

The Bendix–Martin Marietta takeover crisis resulted in new business strategies for both companies that might otherwise have taken a long time to develop. Martin Marietta, which had to pay dearly to escape the clutches of Bendix's Bill Agee, quickly moved to get rid of its sluggish aluminum and construction aggregates businesses. The company's executives did so to reduce some of the debt incurred in the battle with Bendix, but now admit the divisions were not a very good fit within the corporation in the first place. If Agee had succeeded with the takeover, he too planned to sell them off.

Bendix has become part of Allied-Signal, which altered its strategy to integrate the assets it acquired from Bendix. Other instances of new strategies emerging from crises can be seen in the results of the Gulf–Mesa Petroleum–

Chevron battle; the CBS–Ted Turner affair, and the TWA–Frank Lorenzo–Carl Icahn triangle. In each of these cases, the crisis made a strategic change not only possible but desirable. A crisis presents a wonderful opportunity to tear up an old strategic plan and draft a better one.

Early Warning Systems

Most people who have survived a crisis want to find a way to avoid repeating the experience. We like to have control over our lives, personally and in business. But having control necessitates being able to influence events, and to influence events, we need to know what is coming.

To do so, we must establish early warning systems that will sense nonperformance and telegraph trouble long before a crisis starts. Most often a warning during the precrisis period is all that is needed to minimize, if not head off entirely, a developing problem.

The Bank of Boston had many such warnings before its crisis over illegal unreported foreign funds' transfers and cash activities involving gangland characters became public. Banks are highly regulated institutions subject to so many rules and regulations that the Bank of Boston's managers complained that it was hard to tell whether some were not being followed correctly. One can tell, though, and the bank's 1985 crisis showed the need for doing so.

The bank now has a special regulation-assurance team made up of over a hundred people to signal nonperformance early in the game and to correct any faults. In addition, the bank has imposed a "know your customer" policy that will restrict accounts to people of acceptable character. It is unlikely that the Bank of Boston will again be the scapegoat of a federal agency seeking to pull a whole industry into line. The early warning system is in place and should do the job.

The automobile companies are now well equipped for early product crisis detection. Since the mid 1960s, when regulations affecting motor vehicles began to proliferate and recalls became a way of life, the car makers have implemented sophisticated systems to detect product failures and to deal with them quickly. Now they all have electronic information retrieval systems that can quickly flag field problems of any consequence in addition to the older, slower method of collecting data on warranty claims.

New Competitive Edges

The company that survives a crisis is usually smarter and tougher for the experience. Even if it has been temporarily weakened by the experience or reduced in size, its people will reflect the tenacity that got them through.

The ordeal of the crisis tends to produce an *esprit de corps* among the survivors. They have faced a common enemy and have learned to look out for one another. They know how to handle adversity and stage a comeback. They have seen the value of working hard and working smart. There is no more important formula for success in business than a strong leader backed by a loyal, inspired team.

Levi Strauss had its troubles in the 1970s. The very success its blue jeans and other products had enjoyed in the past had attracted a host of strong competitors just as the demand for many of its products was fading. By the mid 1980s, the company had been trimmed back to fighting shape, with its product lines and distribution channels streamlined and with a clearer focus on the markets it would concentrate on in the future. In addition, it had reverted to the status of a private company so that it could take advantage of planning family strategy without the glare of public disclosure.

Coca-Cola found itself embarrassed by one of the most visible marketing mistakes of modern times. Substituting the "new" Coke for the ninety-nine-year-old formula brought such a rebellion on the part of the public that the company was forced to retreat and revive the old formula as Coke Classic. You can bet that Coke's marketing people are sharper today than before the big flap—and a good bit more humble.

Opportunities occur in clusters. It's common to find them taking place simultaneously, as is revealed in the following table of cases presented in this book.

Extraordinary Opportunities in Crisis

Public Perception	Johnson & Johnson 2,3,6,7	Dayco 2,3,4,7	Union Carbide 2,3,5,6,7	Bank of Boston 2,3,4,6,7 / E. F. Hutton 2,3,4,6,7
Sudden Market Shift	Warner/Atari 2,5	Levi Strauss 2,3,5,7	Philip Morris Miller Beer 7	E. F. Johnson CB Radios 2,5
Product Failure	A. H. Robins/Dalkon 2,3	P & G/Rely 2,3	Schlitz Beer 2,3,4,5	Coca-Cola 3,6,7
Management Succession	United Technologies 2,3,4	Occidental Petrol 4	Lehman Bros. 2,3,4,5	
Cash Crisis	Chrysler Corp. 1,2,3,4,7	Wickes 1,2,3,4,7	Wheeling Steel 2,3,4,7	
Industrial Relations Crisis	International Harvester 1,2,3,4,5,7	Pan Am 2,3,5,7		
Hostile Takeover	Bendix/Martin Marietta 2,3,4,5	Gulf/Mesa/Chevron 2,3,4,5,6,7	CBS/Ted Turner 3,5,6	TWA/Icahn 2,3,4,5,7
International Events	GM/OPEC 2,3,4,5,6,7	Caterpillar Tractor 2,3,4,5,7		
Regulation/Deregulation	Braniff 1,2,3,4,5,6,7	Home State Savings Bank 1,2,3,5,6	Western Union 2,3,4,5	Continental Airlines 1,2,3,4,5,7

Legend: (1) Heroes Are Born (2) Change Is Accelerated (3) Problems Are Faced (4) People Are Changed (5) New Strategies Evolve (6) Early Warning Systems Constructed (7) Competitive Edges Sharpened

PART TWO

The Nine Forms of Crises

4

Public Perception
"How Do I Look?"

JOHN DELOREAN was up next. The room holding the American Motors board meeting was hushed except for some nervous muttering. I knew that if DeLorean was convincing enough, he would be the next boss. The door opened; the savior appeared.

He was a vision in Gucci loafers, a fine Italian-tailored suit, and locks of hair that were tousled just enough to avoid looking set. Slim and elegant, he succeeded in relaxing even those of us who saw our life ambitions about to be destroyed. It was an impressive performance, and it almost worked.

During the mid seventies, AMC began planning to replace its top management team. Since 1975, William McNealy and I had been top contenders, believing ourselves safe in that position unless an outsider with better prospects appeared on the scene. Late in the fall of 1976, a special board meeting was called in New York City, and McNealy and I were summoned. I knew it was close to decision time. But I did not know that John DeLorean, who had made an enormous splash three years earlier by abruptly quitting as a group vice president of General Motors, allegedly over matters of principle, was involved until I got to New York. At that point I realized that all he had to do to get the job was sweet-talk the board and come up with a reasonable plan to merge our company with his then-promising sports car project.

His performance was so good that Bill McNealy and I figured we had lost. In the end, though, the board decided to by-pass DeLorean. He wanted too much to merge us with his fledgling company, and it was not entirely clear what the board would be buying. For all his talk of an "ethical sports car," the most we could find in a modeling shop near Detroit was a collection of prototype parts. In retrospect, it is astonishing that he got as close to the top job at AMC as he did.

One lesson I learned from the incident was that how you look counts a whole hell of a lot! AMC's directors were impressed, of course, by DeLorean's track record at GM and his rapid rise to the executive suite on the fourteenth floor of the General Motors Building. But they were even more tantalized by the image he would create for our company; he was Lancelot, whose name alone could connote style and sell cars.

For years DeLorean had been a darling of the press: he had turned from a caterpillar in his earlier jobs at Packard and Chrysler to a butterfly at GM. The only other Detroit figure that got anywhere near the media attention was Lee Iacocca, then at Ford. But if Iacocca was admired, DeLorean was loved, for his panache and the way he was seen to have defied the mighty Corporation. When he left GM, he had accumulated so much personal capital that he seemed destined to succeed at anything he tried. He looked good, and that is what mattered. And he might still be soaring if he had not, as he now admits, tripped over his own ego.

If a good public image can go a long way toward promoting a business career, the reverse is also true. It can be tremendously damaging for a company to have its reputation come under attack in the news media. Even one negative article in *The New York Times* or *The Wall Street Journal* will set off fireworks in the executive suite.

Decisions Under Stress

Most unflattering media stories have a basis in fact, even if all the details may not be right, but once a company has been identified as a bad guy, the beating it takes is out of all proportion as the media, in their competitive battle, fight for new angles and scoops. Television audiences seem to rejoice when a corporation is cast as a villain. And I must confess that I pay more attention to crises than the sort of routine success stories most businessmen prefer to tell.

When a company gets into trouble, and the trouble is made public, the way its executives manage the release of information and handle themselves in dealing with the media can be as important as their business decisions. Even if the amounts of money involved do not threaten the life of the corporation, the damage to its reputation will have serious consequences. Maybe it is the post-Watergate syndrome, but the media and government regulatory agencies are extremely sensitive to anything resembling a cover-up.

Once a scandal breaks, a CEO is usually inundated with conflicting advice. The company's own public relations man, often a former member of the press, usually counsels openness. Deal with the issue forthrightly, he says, and the fuss will be over quickly. Retreating behind a stone wall will only raise suspicions that more lurid misdeeds remain to be discovered. Outside p.r. advisers give similar advice: full disclosure will end the story quickly and limit the damage. This is the time when the company should appoint a single spokesman, reducing the chance of contradictory statements, and have him recite the approved text until the restless media find something else to grab their attention.

The corporate legal advisers will take just the opposite tack. By training and experience they are determined to manage the appearance of innocence. For them, information is a commodity to be bartered. Decline comment, they say, and save everything for the battle in the courtroom or the privacy of negotiations. Smart executives are not intimidated by lawyers who don't have to run the business once the legal skirmishing is over. Trying to minimize or hush up an event can do just the opposite, blowing it up to major proportions in the public's mind — as William Brown of the Bank of Boston discovered to his chagrin.

BANK OF BOSTON

My first meeting with Bill Brown in 1981 was devastating. He sat impassively behind his mammoth carved-oak desk at the Bank of Boston building while I explained why AMC was about to slip into technical default on a $150 million credit agreement. It appeared that he didn't understand my company or the problems facing the twenty-five thousand people depending on it for a living. As president of the bank, he had bigger fish to fry. He explained, "I've got a problem with a huge oil tanker credit." That clearly took priority over a failing automobile company.

We did find a way to avoid bankruptcy. We had already sold a substantial portion of AMC's stock to Renault, and in one final act of desperation I asked our partners in France for some help. Neither they nor we wanted the adverse press that would result from a default or — worse — a loan recall, and they came up with a $75 million bridge loan that cured our fiscal disease.

The incident, though, said something about Brown's style of leadership. Though he was tough, he was not prepared for the spotlight of publicity. He was the classic example of the manager whose idea of leadership was to run the internal operations of the bank for maximum profitability regardless of what others thought. Unlike some of his peers, Brown had little but scorn for the media, and tended to isolate himself from junior bank officers. Thus, for all the bank's deserved reputation for astute business judgment, its top management was not prepared to deal with the disclosure of wrongdoing, even though its lawyers had been negotiating for months with federal authorities. Ira Stepanian, Brown's successor as president, is better cast for his role as crisis manager if trouble breaks out again. He confessed to my class, "We didn't anticipate it well. . . . It's hard to believe it happened." Stepanian is a calm, outgoing, sensitive executive. He rationalized the earlier stonewalling by saying that "we were not going to drag our employees into the limelight for the sake of the media."

The crisis at the Bank of Boston climaxed in early February 1985, when bank officials pleaded guilty to shifting $1.22 billion in cash from overseas without notifying the Internal Revenue Service. At first, Brown tried to dismiss the offenses, as a simple administrative foul-up; a "systems failure," he called it. In crisis management jargon, it was nonperformance and denial in the precrisis phase.

The reason the government in 1970 had started demanding that cash transactions of over $10,000 be reported, and in 1980 had stiffened the reporting requirements, is that international trade in illegal drugs is financed by cash, often with the help of banks. Making banks report large cash transactions was to be a tool in the government's war against drug trafficking, and authorities did not view the Bank of Boston's misdeed as a simple bureaucratic stumble.

Before the guilty plea, Brown had given only two press interviews in the thirteen years since he had been named president of the bank in 1971. Four days after the plea was filed and the maximum $500,000 fine paid, Brown held his first full-blown press conference. It went badly, to say the least. Brown was unyielding and unrepentant. The whole problem, he explained, was the avalanche of government regulations that left bankers unsure of the actual requirements. Even a $1.00 fine was too much for the "simple mistake" of accepting cash without filing reports to the IRS. There were no unsavory implications. What was everybody getting excited about?

But it didn't take long for the complete story to come out, and Brown's attempts to minimize the first disclosure made the details even more titillating. Federal regulators from the office of the comptroller of the currency were able to show that they had repeatedly reminded the bank of the reporting requirements and in 1982 had even subjected it to a special audit of currency transfers.

The bank's second error got it into more trouble; the crisis was spinning out of control. It turned out that the bank's North End branch accepted cash and laundered the money by issuing cashier's checks in return. The sources of most of the cash were the businesses run by Gennaro Angiulo, the alleged head of organized crime in Boston. Moreover, officials of that branch had arbitrarily put the Angiulo companies in the category of privileged or exempt businesses — such as supermarkets that routinely handled large amounts of cash — not required to report cash transactions to the government.

Brown refused to accept blame; he was still in the denial phase. At a later news conference, he acknowledged the Angiulo connection, but said that exempting them from the reporting requirement was only "poor judgment" on the part of some low-level employees. "We are not in the law enforcement business," sniffed a bank spokesman.

Brown's clumsy efforts to manipulate the news media and the public's perception of how the Bank of Boston was managed backfired. The climax of the crisis was at hand. "The bank pleads guilty to 'willfully and knowingly' committing a felony, but contends that it was merely negligent," *The New York Times* commented in an editorial. "That inconsistency strains the bank's credibility with the public." *The Wall Street Journal* was even blunter: Brown's tactics had "demonstrated an almost tragic capacity to make a bad situation worse."

The result was uproar and something approaching panic among the bank's management. Though the $500,000 fine amounted to only a few cents a share in earnings, the bank's stock price quickly dropped from $47 a share to under $42. "If you're a pension manager, you don't want controversial names in your portfolio," one securities analyst observed. Congressional and state banking committees scheduled hearings, and the press was full of cartoons lampooning the blue-blooded bank's relationship with alleged gangsters. Some smaller Massachusetts towns withdrew their deposits in protest. John Walker, a treasury official, claimed there was little doubt that the bank likely was laundering drug money.

With the bank's reputation on the line, the board of directors was forced to try to manage the crisis. A five-member committee of outside directors was appointed to review the entire affair. Its job, in the words of George R. West, an insurance company chairman who headed the panel, was to "take this case from the teller through the whole reporting chain and see . . . where it broke down and if any individual is personally responsible."

The Commitee's judgment was stern. "The bank exhibited widespread laxity and poor judgment in its failures to comply with the cash reporting law," it said in a report issued a few months later. The entire management system was criticized, including Brown, who, the directors said, "must bear some responsibility" for the violations because he "could have taken further steps to ensure that he was kept fully informed by subordinates" of the bank's compliance efforts after the government's investigation began.

The Bank of Boston crisis was slow in building but went through a typical precrisis phase. There was nonperformance — not outright chicanery, if the board's report is accurate — in the repeated failure of lower-level officials to understand the seriousness of the federal cash-reporting requirements and to take action to comply with them. There was nonperformance on the part of more senior managers in not responding to notices from federal officials that they were monitoring the bank's cash transactions. With all the advance warning, Brown should not have been surprised by the flood of publicity that accompanied the guilty plea.

His defensive attitude with the press and the futile effort to conceal the arrangements with the Angiulo family only served to make the public's perception of the bank worse. The media were now "justified" in suggesting that if this much was revealed over the strenuous objections of the leaders of so huge and intimidating an institution, might not much more remain concealed? Bank regulators were delighted. They had landed a big offender to use as an example to other banks who had been lax in enforcing the regulations. "We knew they [the Treasury] needed an example," Stepanian said. "They were not going to let go of this one. We were the stalking horse for the industry."

The crisis was essentially unmanaged until the board stepped in and called for the outside investigation. That step was critical in controlling the situation.

The immediate crisis has passed, but the pain felt by the Bank of Boston is intense. Its reputation has been sullied, and reputation counts for a great deal when a bank woos new corporate customers. The bank is under inspection by regulators and investigators and will have less freedom to maneuver than before. The effect of the crisis on recruiting bright young executives is unmeasurable but doubtlessly depressing. A problem that could have been handled as a private, technical matter between the bank and its regulators, if the warning signals had been heeded, was allowed to grow into a major violation. The eleventh-hour action by the board just managed to stave off collapse.

DAYCO

Richard J. Jacob is chairman of Dayco Corporation, a near $1-billion-a-year, Dayton-based producer of rubber and plastic products. He is an extroverted, voluble, back-slapping super salesman who has twice been listed by *Fortune* magazine as one of the toughest bosses in the country. He appeared before my graduate business school class at Carnegie-Mellon wearing baggy pants and a black knit sweater but no tie. Nor did he polish his words. During his most entertaining talk, he claimed to have developed "thick lips from ass-kissing my customers."

But all his agilities didn't prevent Dayco from falling victim to a swindle, and Jacob's harsh manner in dealing with subordinates didn't give him much practice in burnishing his image when he came under public attack. Like Brown, he had chosen to avoid press contact until he had to meet the media under the worst of circumstances.

Dayco was duped, and Jacob was accused, falsely, as it developed, of taking $3 million in kickbacks in return for accepting over $100 million in orders that later turned out to be phony and cost the company $23.7 million in pretax earnings. He had to defend himself against inquiries by outside directors and federal agencies, shareholder lawsuits, and rumors on Wall Street that worse was to come. As in the Bank of Boston case, the financial losses were easily sustainable, but the effects on the public's view of the company were more serious.

Jacob's problems began when Edith Reich, an international sales agent based in New York, contacted the company in the spring of 1979. Claiming excellent contacts in the Soviet Union, she offered to increase sharply Dayco's sales to the Soviets. By November she had landed an order for $1.7 million worth of V-belts, used to transmit power in industrial machinery. With the company's automotive customers pulling back because of a recession, Jacob was eager to try an untapped market.

Jacob signed up Reich as the company's exclusive sales agent in the Soviet Union and agreed to pay her a 10 percent advance commission on all orders she placed, overruling subordinates who argued that the commission was too high and that the company had never paid commissions before getting paid itself. By late 1980, Dayco had $114 million in orders from Reich and was busily churning out the goods and shipping them to warehouses on the German coast, where they were supposed to be picked up by Russian freighters. Little alarm bells were going off, but Jacob ignored them. Most of the shipments lay gathering dust in the warehouses, and payments from Reich were only trickling in.

When Jacob tried to force the issue in December 1980 by refusing to pay any more commissions, Reich threatened to stop all orders and payments. Jacob backed down and continued the arrangement, despite some questions from his auditors about the advance payments. He said he attributed the slowness of payment to a lack of foreign currency in the Soviet Union due to the invasion of Afghanistan and general East-West tensions.

Before the end of the following year, it was obvious within the company that Dayco was in trouble. It had already manufactured $47 million worth of products and had received only $6 million in payments from Reich. Worse, it had paid her over $13 million in commissions. The outside directors were so concerned that they hired a company specializing in trade with the Soviets to investigate the validity of Reich's orders. Early in 1982 Dayco took the bitter medicine and wrote off the Soviet orders, slashing its reported profit of $9 million for 1981 to a loss of $2.7 million. The unmanaged crisis was peaking, and the pain level was at its highest.

Following press accounts of the swindle, three shareholder suits were filed, seeking damages from Dayco and the board of directors. When Dayco filed a fraud suit against Reich, she countersued, charging that Jacob had got $3 million in kickbacks and had tried to extort another $1 million from her. He had known all along that the Russian orders were fictitious, she said. She claimed that other Dayco officials had taken kickbacks as well, and the truth of those charges, uncovered later, gave credibility to her other claims.

Jacob insisted on treating the affair as an ordinary business loss, despite his being viewed by the public as a boss who lined his pockets from company coffers. He said he was treated "horribly" by the media, but on the advice of his lawyers he kept silent while allegations of insider-trading violations and shaky dealing circulated.

Finally, in June 1982, Jacob launched a counteroffensive. He gave interviews to *The New York Times* and *The Wall Street Journal*. His message was direct: the company was basically sound and would survive the losses of the Reich affair. Her commissions were prepaid, he said, "because that was the only way we could get the orders" at a time when sales were slumping badly. All he had personally received from Reich was a coin commemorating the 1980 Moscow Olympic games and some Russian caviar that "was served in the company lunchroom." As a major stockholder in Dayco, what did he have to gain from stealing from himself?

He traveled to all of Dayco's offices in the United States to answer the questions of worried local managers and to assure them that he had the complete support of the board of directors. This was not very surprising, since he had hand-picked almost every member of the board. Still, the eight outside directors felt obliged to launch an investigation of Jacob's role in the affair, as well as that of other Dayco executives.

By August, they had concluded that Jacob was innocent of personal wrongdoing, but two high-ranking officers were fired for taking payments from Reich. Two years later, the courts ruled in Dayco's favor, finding Reich liable for $19 million in damages, although the company would be able to collect only a small fraction of that amount, because she had gone into personal bankruptcy. In addition, Reich was subsequently arrested and charged with fraud by new federal authorities. The automobile business rebounded, and Dayco's sales and earnings increased sharply, erasing most of the effects of the whole bungle.

Jacob survived the crisis, despite the initial mismanagement, but says he still bears the scars. In part, his situation was caused by his own poor judgment in grasping at uncertain orders in a panicky attempt to get new business. Everything was worsened by his inability to manage the problem when it burst open in public. His first reaction was to continue business as usual, managing the company as before and delegating the crisis to staff members, who themselves were in conflict about how to act. He was aggressive in dealing with known quantities, such as his employees, customers, and suppliers, but his view of outsiders, particularly the news media, was that they were all "bastards" out to ruin him and his company.

Public perception crises have a particularly shattering effect on top management. The very visibilty of the situation interferes with rational thought. It is bad enough to have a business problem and the internal turmoil that accompanies it, but it is much worse when reporters call with probing questions and the public seems to brand you as a loser or a crook. For those not accustomed to dealing with the press and the public, it can be a bitter experience. The challenge is to end the affair as quickly as possible and limit the damage.

When an organization comes under siege, people's loyalties begin to erode. They feel embarrassed, the way an E. F. Hutton executive felt after the company admitted to what amounted to a check-kiting scam. "I'm frustrated," he told *The New York Times.* "You have to be frustrated when the name of the firm you work for is dragged over the coals day after day." Desertions can become a major problem. Headhunters see a scandal as a signal to start making discreet contacts with your best people.

Board members can also put a lot of pressure on top management to get the company off television and out of newspapers. The directors of Beatrice Corporation finally dropped James L. Dutt as CEO after a long run of bad press caused largely by management defections. The management brain drain was one thing; the attention paid to it quite another. David S. Lewis left after allegations of overcharging on defense contracts appeared in the press. The magnitude of the overcharges was questionable, but not the extent of the abuse heaped on Lewis.

Chief executives can get away with lying to a board of directors, but not with embarrassing them before the public. Dick Jacob embarrassed his board, first by taking the phony orders and then by stonewalling the press. He survived because his business was fundamentally sound, because he had a large measure of control over his board, and because he finally decided to deal with the issue of outside appearances. Contrary to what most businessmen think, the press is not implacably hostile to business or out to "get" corporate leaders. Particularly for a company making consumer products, the press is another constituency; like suppliers, customers, and lenders, it has to be kept satisfied. Successful politicians learned this long ago. They look good because they have convinced the media watchers that they have what it takes.

Devoting care to appearances is a proper function of management. It is surprising that capable executives, who take pride in their adroitness in smoothing a lender's ruffled feathers or sweet-talking customers into placing orders, choke up when dealing with the media. After all, it is usually the company that controls the information in a crisis — reporters and editors can only ask questions. The way a situation is presented can have a big impact on the way a story is played.

When Lee Iacocca took over Chrysler, the company had an image of bumbling incompetence. It was run by accountants — "bean counters," in Detroit parlance — who had managed to destroy the company's long-standing reputation for top-quality engineering. But Iacocca was different; he was a "car guy," the father of the famous Mustang. He was articulate and accessible to reporters. When Chrysler was forced to approach the federal government for assistance, Iacocca revealed future product programs and other business plans that had always been treated as secrets in Detroit — even though everyone in the car business usually knew pretty well what the other guys had coming.

Iacocca gave interview after interview, even inviting newspaper publishers to Detroit to hear his sales spiel. He did TV commercials; he wrote off the past and emphasized the future; he handed out bottles of black ink when Chrysler eked out a tiny profit after billions in losses. And perceptions began to change. Even before the company was back on its feet financially, its image was changing from a sluggish, ill-managed producer of rust-prone gas guzzlers to a gutsy underdog trying to take on the big guys against all odds. The people loved it.

This is not to say that Iacocca simply talked Chrysler back to life; he made far-reaching management changes and some savvy product choices. But his deft manipulation of the public's perceptions helped convince drivers to keep buying Chrysler cars, even when it looked as if the company was a goner.

Many managers have the fear of being "ambushed" by the press. Their nightmare is Mike Wallace shoving a microphone in their face and giving them thirty seconds to explain a delicate, complex situation. The solution is to be prepared. It's your business and you are the expert. Be ready for the kinds of questions that are going to be asked and have a quick response. Understand that a television reporter is going to have only sixty or ninety seconds on the air to cover your story, but that the guy from *Time* or *Newsweek* wants all the details. Don't lie, don't stonewall — but don't make things worse by talking too much. No one will fault you for presenting a story from your point of view as long as the facts are correct.

Public Perception and the Public Sector

A common side effect of a public perception crisis is an unwanted increase in attention from the public sector. Regulatory, health, and safety agencies often get into the act, and with them come the special interest groups. Few things are as disruptive to a chief executive's operating style as having to testify at congressional hearings and submit to endless investigations by regulatory agencies. Legislative hearings are a form of theater, designed to enhance the image of the politicians in control. Groups that don't amount to much more than a few people, a letterhead, and a duplicating machine will be given the same attention as the chief executive of a major corporation if that suits the committee chairman's purpose.

The stringency of regulations affecting an industry can tighten overnight as the result of a crisis. The near meltdown at the Three Mile Island nuclear power plant in 1979 brought cries for tougher supervision of plants still under construction. The Nuclear Regulatory Commission responded by demanding full documentation of each step of construction at the incredibly complex plants. For many of the projects, it was a death blow. Under the less stringent regulations in force before the Three Mile Island incident, filing documents was subordinate to keeping projects on schedule. Many managers could not produce the needed records, and the physical evidence, such as welds in pipes, were buried under yards of concrete. Some nuclear plants, such as the Zimmer project in Ohio, were abandoned, not because they were thought to be unsafe, but because their managers did not have the required documents and could not afford to dismantle the plants to create them.

JOHNSON & JOHNSON

As we have seen, most crises in public perception come from internal causes. The fire is fanned by management that acts aloof or is unskilled in dealing with the media. Executives look ignorant or indifferent when they say "No comment." What could appear worse to a public seeking a concerned, personal response? Johnson & Johnson had little experience in dealing with the news media; it went out of its way to avoid publicity. "We had a penchant for no press contact," said David Collins, the company's vice chairman. "In fact, we didn't even talk to Wall Street, but that changed after Tylenol."

One might have expected fireworks when, through no fault of its own, the company was subjected to the glare of public attention brought about by its first unhappy experience with the painkiller Extra Strength Tylenol capsules. There was no way management could have anticipated a madman's lacing bottles of the medicine with deadly poison. The quality of the product itself was not in question, but people were dying, and the company's innocence did not mitigate the distress.

Although J & J could not have anticipated the crisis, it moved swiftly to contain the damage. First, it got organized, set up a crisis team, and pulled all packages of Tylenol off the shelves. Following up quickly, it had the courage to launch the product again in a hastily designed "tamper-resistant" package. The company realized that its lack of fault was no reason to deny that a crisis existed and that corrective action had to be taken. As for its traditional publicity-shy ways, "the issue never came up," Collins explained. The crisis changed J & J permanently and prepared the company to handle the second Tylenol crisis, which followed shortly.

J & J thought that sealing the packages of Tylenol would solve the tampering problem. But it found that little can be done to stop someone bent on adulterating a product for irrational purposes. On February 8, 1986, Dianne Elsroth, twenty-three years old, died after taking a Tylenol capsule that had had poison placed in it. Slammed once again by a highly visible public perception crisis, J & J took decisive action. Production of Tylenol capsules would be ended, it said, to eliminate the danger to the public. Instead, the company would produce "caplets," solid, smooth, capsule-shaped pills that would be hard to contaminate but easy to swallow.

The decision cost the company over $150 million, but it preserved the perception of a company that was responsible and responsive to adverse events. James E. Burke, the chairman of J & J, and Collins were ready for the second crisis. They had learned to take charge quickly, establish the facts, set up a crisis team, select a spokesman, tell their story, and fix the problem. They managed the crisis.

UNION CARBIDE

Shortly after midnight on December 3, 1984, methylisocyanate gas poured out of Union Carbide's plant in Bhopal, India, and the world's worst industrial accident was under way. Over 1500 people were killed by the deadly white vapor, and tens of thousands more were permanently injured. The corporation itself was also severely damaged. It was immediately assaulted by a barrage of damage lawsuits mounting into the billions of dollars, though it had offered from the first to make financial restitution to those involved. It was subjected to unremitting scrutiny by the media and government regulators. The company's stock price wilted, and soon corporate raiders were sniffing around.

The company's own efforts to find out what was happening in Bhopal in those early days were thwarted by clogged telephone lines and overbooked airplanes. Warren

Anderson, the chairman of Carbide, was aghast at initial reports that sixty people had died. The actual magnitude of the horror wasn't known until several days after the accident.

Three months later, Anderson told a news conference that conditions at the plant were so bad that "we shouldn't have been operating." Blaming the tragedy on the Indians who operated the facility, he said "Safety is the responsibility of the people who operate the plants." The parent company in the United States, he said, was not responsible for the problems in Bhopal.

The lawyers who flocked to Bhopal to represent clients were unimpressed, as were the Indian government and American regulatory agencies. Carbide, which had struggled for years to clean up its reputation as a polluter, was in the midst of a public perception crisis that shook the company to its foundations. Although Anderson flew to India to try to take control of the situation, the company's general response was to stay behind closed corporate doors and toss out an occasional press release to the media representatives camped outside. This didn't make the problem go away; it only made things worse. Anderson, a gracious and warmhearted man who is easy to like and comfortable to be with, argues that he didn't know enough to talk — at least at the start. "If you say something before you really know the facts, you speculate," he said. "If it is subsequently wrong, you are a liar. If you don't say anything, you are a stonewaller." But by appearing not to be forthcoming and sensitive to the horror at Bhopal, Carbide set itself up for intense criticism.

The New York Times took sharp note of the contrast between Carbide's defensiveness and the immediate resignation of Yasumoto Takagi, the president of Japan Airlines, after the tragic crash of one of its aircraft claimed 520 lives. "Union Carbide's defensive posture and faceless approach surely reflect a desire to limit liability in anticipation of lawsuits," it said. "Mr. Takagi's response, on the other hand, was dictated by the Japanese sense of personal responsibility." This sense of responsibility, the *Times* went on to say, "has much to do with the success of Japanese industry, a point American managers might ponder."

The Bhopal crisis, though it burst unexpectedly, was not without warning. As usual, there was nonperformance by low-level managers, in this case the operators of the Bhopal plant. A company audit in 1982 warned about problems at the facility, but top management's attention was focused elsewhere. Mr. Anderson was trying to reorient the company from its historic dependence on commodity chemicals, like the pesticides produced at Bhopal, toward consumer products, like the Glad plastic bags, Eveready batteries, and Prestone antifreeze it was already marketing. Those at the top were concentrating on strategic planning, not operations.

As a subsequent study found, much of the equipment at the Indian plant was faulty or inoperative, so when the deadly gas began to escape there was no means to contain it. And Carbide's local managers, under political pressure in a crowded country, had permitted housing to be built right next to the plant, despite the huge quantities of toxic chemicals being handled there.

Nor were all the instances of nonperformance in India, as Anderson discovered nearly eight months later, when there was a serious leak at the company's facility in Institute, West Virginia. Six operators found themselves engulfed by toxic gas with only two gas masks between them. A hundred of the plant's neighbors were sent to the hospital; the townspeople were understandably apprehensive. Nobody died, but more broken equipment was found, as was evidence of a lack of attention to safety standards. The company reacted more rapidly this time, having learned from the Bhopal incident. Aided by the vastly better communications in the United States, it assessed the situation and issued statements as quickly as the facts became known. A final report came out in weeks, rather than months, helping to put the matter to rest.

Still, Anderson seemed uncomfortable with the public's continuing concern about the apparent neglect of safety at Carbide. "Today, you couldn't invent the pencil," he fumed. "Children use them and they have sharp points." But belittling safety concerns does not make them go away or enhance the public's regard for a company.

At this writing, Carbide is reeling from the aftershocks of its largely unmanaged crisis. Lawsuits amounting to billions of dollars still threaten. Legislators are proposing to tighten the regulations imposed on chemical plants, which can only squeeze profit margins. The company was viewed on Wall Street for a while as a prime candidate for a hostile attack and dismemberment. In response to a takeover attempt by Sam Heyman of GAF, it has decided to liquidate its commercial products' division — a $2 billion-a-year enterprise — and return the proceeds to the shareholders. UC may never recover from its multiple crises and now seems destined to survive as a ho-hum producer of chemical products and to remain deeply in debt.

Lessons from Perception Crises

Carbide was in serious trouble as soon as the deadly gas began to leak in Bhopal, but there were some steps that it, Dayco, and the Bank of Boston could have taken to limit the damage from their crises.

First, management should have been in charge early and pinpointed the problem. If the bank had struck a deal with the government over cash transfers before the amounts swelled into millions, if Dayco had demanded authentication from Edith Reich before filling orders, and if UC had invested in safety equipment at Bhopal and Institute, the cost to the companies would have been far less after each crisis peaked.

Next, once a crisis arose, particularly one involving public perceptions, the wise chief executive would have sought an outsider's opinion on how his actions would appear to the public. No one inside any organization has the perspective, and the independence, to do so. What with the public relations staff advising the CEO to hang out all the dirty linen at once and the lawyers trying to keep a lid on everything but the most self-serving disclosures, it would have taken an outsider to weigh the two views and suggest a wiser course.

There is a strong tendency for executives caught in situations like these to argue about the difference between "perception" — the way the world sees what's going on — and "reality" — the way he sees it. In fact, there is no gap between appearance and reality. Reality is what the public perceives to be true, and if the public grasps reality in a certain way, that is what it becomes. Reality is what your customers, suppliers, bankers, regulators, and other constituencies believe. But what about scientific truth, facts that can be proven? They don't apply. Most commercial crises are not subject to repeatability or laboratory tests under controlled conditions to establish "truth."

How you look — as an individual and as a corporation — does count. Dick Jacob was right when he asserted that Dayco easily had the capacity to absorb the losses from the Reich affair. But if he had moved more swiftly to manage the crisis and his participation in it, the damage to his personal reputation would have been greatly reduced.

5

Sudden Market Shift
"Which Way Did They Go?"

REMEMBER THE PACER, the short, wide car with the big windows? I sure do. Its successful beginning and sudden demise tell a story that reaches beyond the life and death of a single product.

Long lead times are the bane of the automobile industry. Because basic decisions on products have to be made three to four years before a car hits the market, you're out of luck if the market shifts in the meantime. That's why the car companies looked so stupid in the early 1980s. In the late 1970s the public was clamoring for big cars; Ford was even rationing V-8 engines. Then in 1979, OPEC restricted the amount of oil exported to the United States, and long lines formed at gas stations. Suddenly the public wanted fuel-efficient cars, but all Detroit had to supply were the lumbering boats that top executives had approved during the big-car boom times. Only in the mid 1980s did they manage to adjust to a changed market.

This sort of shift had happened before, to our detriment

at AMC. The Pacer was introduced in January 1975, during a recession, and it took off. The market response to the unusual car was fantastic. AMC dealers could not remember seeing so much traffic in their showrooms, as prospective buyers streamed in to look at this new idea in automotive transportation. Forget the economic crunch; American Motors had created a miracle car. Our production lines strained to meet the demand.

Nine months later it was all over. Sales had fallen from twelve thousand a month to under half that number. What had gone wrong? What could possibly have caused a car to sell like crazy and then drop dead? As William Pickett, our general sales manager at the time, said, "We went a hundred and twenty miles an hour for two inches."

The market had changed. The first fuel crisis, in 1973, had made fuel economy a hot item. The Pacer promised that feature but, for reasons beyond our control, could not deliver it. The first wave of buyers saw a small car — which seemed to imply great fuel economy — with the roominess of a big one. Then came the realization that the Pacer really didn't have the gas mileage that the imports from Japan had.

It shouldn't have been that way. The key to the Pacer was the small but powerful Wankel rotary engine, invented in Germany and being developed further by General Motors, that would produce extraordinary power from a small, light package. With it, we could design a car that would weigh two thousand pounds, have a two-liter engine, and sell for $2000. Ed Cole, the president of GM, had promised to sell us the engine. (Sales of components between automobile companies are common, though they are not advertised. Selling 150,000 or 200,000 engines a year to AMC would stretch out GM's production run and improve the economics of the project.)

Something went wrong, though. GM was unable to

overcome technical problems with the Wankel, and the project was shelved. The decision was a small matter for GM but a tragedy for AMC. We were forced to substitute the only engine we could make on our own, a massive old six-cylinder job. The huge engine forced a complete redesign of the car, and we wound up with a vehicle that weighed three thousand pounds, had a five-liter engine, and cost $3500. When the market tilted toward greater fuel economy, the Pacer died.

Those Shifty Markets

Sometimes it is amazing how fast a market can slip away from you. You expect fad products, like Hula Hoops and Pet Rocks, to blaze up and disappear. But other, more fundamental markets can slip away just as quickly and well-planned products and marketing organizations — whole corporations, in fact — find themselves high and dry.

When a market changes abruptly, there is nothing subtle about the effect; there is plenty of public attention to the big names tumbling down. Those that are hot as a pistol today wind up on the discounters' back shelves when public tastes change.

CB radios had been around for a long time and were mainly used by hobbyists and long-haul truckers. Then suddenly, in the late 1970s, everyone seemed to want one. A new era of citizen communication appeared to be dawning. We would never be alone again. We were going to talk to each other all day from our cars, our homes, and our offices. "O.K., good buddy" and "10-4" became part of our language. Producers sprang up everywhere, domestically and overseas. Sales went from a dribble to millions of units. Federal officials were afraid that the airwaves would become so crowded as to be useless, and they tried to see that every set was licensed, but the volume was too big and they finally gave up.

Today, if there is any problem with CBs, it is not how many people are using them but what they are saying on them. The market has so diminished over the last few years that it is once again almost the private province of over-the-road truckers talking to one another in their distinctive argot. The profanity turns the air blue — not that most people care.

The CB radio was too much a marketing and production event to be called a fad. It was an extreme example of a shift in public interest that went unexplained, and it devastated many companies, like E. F. Johnson and Motorola, that hopped on the bandwagon, only to find it plunging off a cliff.

The crisis of sudden market shift is the hardest for a manager to predict and one of the most difficult to control. Unlike a public perception crisis, where decisive, quick action can limit the damage, the sudden expiration of a market leaves your warehouses bulging with unwanted products, and there is not much immediate action you can take.

ATARI

Few markets have shifted as quickly as that for video games, as Steven Ross of Warner Communications discovered to his chagrin. Ross had built Warner into a conglomeration of businesses that sold leisure-time products ranging from movies to computers to perfumes. He didn't believe in overmanaging the creative people who developed new products, and ran the company as a decentralized operation with entrepreneurial flair. His approach seemed to work. By emphasizing home entertainment products, which complemented Warner's other businesses, he steadily boosted profits and made the stock such a hot property that it shot from $1.87 a share to over $60 a share in just six years in the late 1970s.

His willingness to take a risk led Warner in 1976 to buy the faltering Atari company from its founder, Nolan Bushnell, for $28 million. Bushnell had cash-flow problems and was trying to interest a range of buyers; Warner made the deal because nobody else was really interested. At that point, neither Atari's video computer system (VCS) nor a similar product from Odyssey — then a subsidiary of Magnavox — was doing particularly well. But then Atari licensed the game Space Invaders, which had been pulling in the quarters at video arcades, for home use, and VCS sales took off. Within five years of Warner's purchase, Atari was selling $900 million a year in products and throwing off $250 million in profit. By 1981 it accounted for 25 percent of Warner's sales and 57 percent of its operating profit, controlled 70 percent of the video game market, and looked like a license to print money well into the future. The very name *Atari* became synonymous with advanced, technically savvy thinking. The "Atari Democrats" of the 1984 presidential campaign were those willing to break with the traditions that had led the party to its first stunning defeat at the hands of Ronald Reagan.

But Atari's success had attracted a lot of attention — and competition. New entrants in the market began besting Atari at hardware, software, manufacturing, and marketing. Mattel jumped into the market in 1980 with Intellivision, a more sophisticated machine whose operating system was incompatible with Atari's. Pushed by author George Plimpton's witty television commercials, and boasting better graphics and more complex games than Atari, Intellivision grabbed the top end of the video game market.

Atari struck back with its 5200 series, which were

slightly more sophisticated than Intellivision, but were not compatible with either its major rival or with older Atari machines. That meant that established Atari customers couldn't run their Pac-Man and other cartridges on the new device; the gaffe tested — and lost — customer loyalty. Meanwhile other companies began producing machines that could be inexpensively adapted to run Atari cartridges. Then the price of home computers, which could perform serious operations as well as play games, began to fall, leaving Atari a relatively low-tech entry in a market that was moving toward more advanced technology.

The customer who went shopping for a video game wound up buying a computer, because often the difference in price was less than $100. Atari's managers, out of touch with their customers' changing attitudes and lulled by their early success, were slow to respond to the changing market with the upgraded products and aggressive pricing needed to recapture the initiative. By December 1982, the precrisis period was ending and the crisis was at hand. Early in the month, Warner's management had assured analysts that the fourth quarter was going to be as strong as expected and predicted a 50 percent increase in profits for the year. Then they changed their tune; there had been a slight miscalculation, they said. Profits would be up only 10 percent or so. The news sent a shiver through the stock market, and the price of Warner's shares plunged to $32 a share within a week. *Fortune* magazine reported that "an inside joke at Warner is that Atari's next hit video game will be named 'Margin Call.'"

Time began to run out. Of the top twenty programmers who had been working for Atari when Warner acquired it, only four remained by 1982. The company was in a poor position to compete in a rapidly changing market. Steve Ross reacted the following year by hiring James J. Morgan away from Philip Morris to try to turn the operation around. Morgan ordered a thirty-day freeze on product development and product introductions while he learned the business. Although this move was probably to be expected from a take-charge manager, it blew the 1983 Christmas season for Atari and delayed the introduction of the more sophisticated 1450 XLD machine until June 1984.

Atari's loss of $539 million in 1983 was pulling Warner under, and its depressed stock price soon began attracting corporate sharks. Rupert Murdoch, the publishing tycoon, began quietly buying up Warner stock and had amassed 8.5 percent before he announced his holdings in a filing with the Securities and Exchange Commission in December 1983. Warner, looking for a white knight to defeat Murdoch, allowed Chris Craft Industries to take control of 29 percent of its stock, but still found it necessary to buy out the Australian press lord. Warner had to pay Murdoch $31 a share, a 30 percent premium over the price at the time, and cover his $8 million in legal costs as well. Almost as damaging as the expense was the diversion of management attention from running the business to fending off the possible takeover.

There were other signs of disarray. Two of Steve Ross's subordinates were prosecuted for illegally taking payments from a slush fund, and it soon became clear that the ultimate target was Ross himself. He was never formally accused, but the unwanted attention took its toll. In August 1984 Warner sold Atari to Jack Tramiel for $240 million in notes that will have little value unless the company can be nursed back to financial health.

The Atari case had all the markings of an unmanaged crisis. Warner had no clear idea of what was driving the video game market nor did it notice when the market quickly began to change. No one there was sure whether video games were a fad or would become a permanent fixture in American life. "Pac-Man came at the wrong moment, just before the competition in video games heated up," a top Atari executive admitted later. "It lulled us into a false sense of security."

Rather than trying to figure what was happening in the video game business, and devising strategies to minimize future damage, Atari's management reacted by plunging into the home computer business without knowing much about it or possessing any competitive advantage. Ross hired a cigarette marketer, who was thoroughly unfamiliar with Warner, as his savior, and Morgan failed. In the end, he all but gave Atari away. That is one way to end a crisis. It is also an example of the terminal stage of an unmanaged crisis — radical change.

LEVI STRAUSS

Market shifts are not restricted to products of high technology. Long-established products can get hot unexpectedly and cool off just as fast. Levi Strauss found his fortune in the gold fields of Northern California in the last century by selling denim trousers that were durable even for miners panning for riches in cold mountain streams. The company that bore his name became identified with blue jeans, which are referred to in many parts of the country simply as Levi's.

It was a steady, if not spectacular, business, and the company marketed a variety of apparel for both men and women. Then, in the mid 1970s, jeans became fashionable. Sales soared, and Levi Strauss had 25 percent of the market, nearly three times the share of its nearest rival, Wrangler. Revenues increased from $1.2 billion in 1976 to

$2.8 billion four years later, an astonishing compound growth rate of 24 pecent. The company strained to meet the growing demand, and by 1980 had eleven new production plants and five distribution centers in various stages of completion.

Levi Strauss had diversified somewhat from its core blue jeans market; about a third of its sales came from such items as slacks, skirts, jackets, hats, and accessories. Most of its marketing was done through specialty boutiques, jeans stores, and department stores like New York's Macy's. When "designer jeans" were introduced — slightly fancier, more stylishly cut trousers with someone's name or initials on the back pocket — the company decided to ignore them. Just a passing fad, they thought. After all, wasn't the company's motto "Quality never goes out of style"? Rather than introduce a competing signature edition, which they could have easily done, Robert Haas, the president, and the company's other managers figured that Levi's reputation for value and quality would see them through.

It didn't. Levi's amazing growth machine sputtered in 1981 for the first time in eight years. The demand for everyday jeans had leveled out, and the baby boomers who had fueled Levi's sales were moving on to more trendy clothes. What management had seen as a solid and expanding market turned out to be a demographic bulge with fickle taste. Even Levi's fashion lines of apparel were hurt, because most of those items bore the familiar red Levi's tab at a time when buyers were demanding designer labels. The situation was confused by the recession of the early 1980s, which caused retailers to cut orders across the board. Levi's had lasted through previous downturns, but was now being treated as one of the pack. Clearly something fundamental had changed.

After a period of indecision, Levi Strauss managers

reacted. They began to emphasize fashion lines, heavily advertising the 501 jeans line introduced in 1982. They broke with past policy and decided to distribute through mass marketers, like Sears and Penney's. The move alienated many of its past retailers, but it added twenty-six hundred retail outlets. The company closed some of its older plants and, for the first time in its history, laid off people to cut costs. Most important, the company's managers came to realize that, as Robert Haas said, "Just putting the Levi's name on something isn't enough to gain instant marketing acceptance."

The company kept trying to chase its market. In response to requests from retailers, it brought back the David Hunter fashion jeans line, without the Levi's label, after having dropped it in 1980. In 1984, Levi's said it would make designer clothes and ventured into the growing market for athletic wear, promoting the move by outfitting that year's U.S. Olympic team.

Levi Strauss has since changed its focus, broadening from a blue jeans company into an apparel company that will have a wide variety of products to protect it from sudden changes in fashion. The notion that the Levi's name alone could sell clothing was a by-product of the exploding market for blue jeans in the 1970s. When the market shifted, the company's managers found it wasn't so.

Now they realize that Levi Strauss is selling in at least two major markets. The first is for everyday wear, the traditional blue jean market. In signing up Sears and Penney's as retailers, the company recognizes that its prime customers are the men and women of middle America and that the product is basically a commodity. There had been some earlier discussion inside the company about selling through the giant chain stores, but it took a crisis for the decision to be made.

The other market is for fashion apparel, an arena that requires quick reflexes and a keen sensitivity to shifts in fads and tastes. Top company officials are aware that their own style has to change. "This company is guilty of being too rigid and too deliberative in an industry made up of entrepreneurs who hustle," said one key executive.

The pain from Levi Strauss's crisis continues. The Haas family, headed by Robert, the great-great-grandnephew of the founder, was rocked by the roller-coaster ride of its stable business. Indeed, the family decided that the process of extracting itself from misfortune in the full view of public inspection was too much to endure. If a sudden market shift would cause this much trouble and public displeasure, why remain a public company?

In August 1985, by means of one of the largest leveraged buyouts to that point in history, involving more than $1.4 billion, the Haas family reversed what it had done fifteen years earlier: it took the company private, saying the change "would allow management to focus its attention on the long term rather than being concerned with the short term, as a public company must be." A sudden market shift had taken its toll. One of the oldest companies in the apparel business (136 years), with one of the most respected family names in the industry, had withdrawn from public view.

Adjusting to Changing Markets

Many companies experience sudden market shifts. Some are geared to deal with it; many are not. The garment industry lives on change; retailing thrives on it; toy makers depend on it. Yet some industries that are constantly faced with the prospect of changing public taste seem poorly equipped to manage it effectively. In the case of the automobile industry, the reason is twofold. First, it takes time to retool. It is common to spend thirty to thirty-six months getting ready to bring out a new model. More important, though, is momentum. Automobile companies are so large that, like giant oil tankers, they turn very slowly, even when the need is urgent.

For years the automobile companies brought out new models annually and on time; the industry was smug about its ability to keep up with changing markets. As long as evolutionary change was sufficient and the Detroit-based companies controlled the North American market, there was no one to defy their dominance. The gauntlet was thrown down in the 1970s. Imports suddenly became a reasonable alternative to Detroit's products, and a generation of young people fell in love with the reliable, durable, efficient, improved cars from Japan. The market shifted dramatically, and the change found Detroit unable to answer the challenge.

Then the Yom Kippur War between Israel and its Arab neighbors in 1973 led to the first cutoff of oil from the Arab countries that triggered the dramatic change. General Motors was the worst hit, since it depended so heavily on big cars for the bulk of its sales and profits. Never before or since have I seen such fear in the eyes of GM executives. The turn in the market had caught them completely off balance. Even though they had tried to develop a few small car models in this country, sales had been poor and they didn't have the capacity to crank up production quickly.

For AMC it was wonderful. We had a fine reputation as a producer of economy cars, and our sales boomed. But we needed more — we had to have a subcompact car. The problem was that we didn't have one in the works or the means to develop one in time.

On a Northwest Airlines flight between Milwaukee and

Detroit one September afternoon Richard A. (Dick) Teague, our talented chief stylist, pulled out the air-sickness bag and put it on the table between us. The smile on his face made it clear that he wasn't about to be ill. We had been talking about our need for a subcompact and our danger of missing the market. I had said AMC should be first, because economy cars were our specialty. Dick began sketching on the bag. He started by drawing a Hornet; then he chopped twelve inches from the section behind the driver's seat and drew an unusual roof line that was as attractive as it was different. Finally, he wrote a name for the car on a lower corner of the bag — Gremlin. And there was a brand-new idea in car design, conceived and labeled on the back of an airplane "barf bag." The short cuts Teague suggested on paper were brilliant. The normal tooling time for a new model was cut in half and the costs pared sharply. The car was on the market eighteen months later, and AMC became the first domestic auto company to bring out a fuel-efficient subcompact car. The truncated rear end gave it a distinctive appearance that appealed to many buyers. We sold a million Gremlins before phasing out the car ten years later. This was one case where AMC managed to capture a shift in the market to its considerable advantage.

Meeting the challenge of a fast-moving market requires basic and immediate changes in products and strategy. Under Romney it was daring to bring out the first subcompact car; Chapin was daring in buying Jeep and revitalizing it; and I thought it was daring to merge the company with Renault to obtain a new line of lightweight cars for our dealers and ensure our future. The pace quickens. Imports are forcing the auto industry to move at an even faster tempo to stay in step with a rapidly changing market.

* * *

One of the most daunting aspects of a crisis caused by sudden market shift is that it is so hard to manage. When the demand for your product dies, you die. Some industries are particularly susceptible to such shifts; just look at the relationship between automobiles and oil. In high-tech industries, change is expected, so organizations are prepared to react quickly. Others are slower afoot.

Salespeople are often the last to see a shift taking place; they are usually so bent on achieving their objectives that to question their direction draws nothing but scorn. But you can spot these changes early if you're on the lookout. Usually there is a forerunner part of the market that gives off warning signals; in the car business, it is California. Watch that portion of the market or that geographic area with special care for tip-offs.

It is when you are doing so well that you can barely credit it — as was Atari — that you are particularly vulnerable. And that's when you should be checking the early warning devices. Auto executives spend a lot of time talking to dealers, but they seldom learn much from them about what the public feels, because everything is filtered through the dealer's own perspective. Here Peters's and Waterman's advice about having a customer orientation should be taken with caution. The customer for an auto company is the dealer, but he is not the ultimate buyer. If staying close to the customer is the key to success, auto companies would be badly misled by listening only to dealer reaction. Far more important is the end user, the customer's customer — you and I.

The larger the market share a company has, the more vulnerable it is to a sudden market shift. Also, big companies that are cautiously managed — General Motors, Exxon, U.S. Steel, for example — get the worst jolts when conditions change, because they are set in their ways. A company with a long tradition, like Levi Strauss, likewise finds it hard to abandon the formulas for success handed down by the founding fathers. A company that enjoys all three advantages — commanding market share, great girth, and deep roots — should realize its vulnerability.

Most managers think they are prepared to deal with sudden market shifts; business schools have prepared them to be on guard. But often the change takes place when top management is distracted by something else, like the automobile executives who were so wrapped up in devising ways to meet government safety and emissions regulations that they were stunned when the oil crisis hit. When a market starts changing, the temptation is to regard the situation as a "sales group problem" and let the rest of the organization proceed as usual. But when the dogs don't like your dog food, you and everybody in the organization has to figure out what the market is saying and how to face the new reality.

Sudden market shift crises tend to linger until the fundamental adjustments have been made. These are hard problems to fix, and to some extent they are beyond a manager's control, at least in the short term. In the long run, you can control your product and your people and make the necessary adjustments — but only if you understand what the public wants.

A heavy burden falls on designers to come up with the product demanded by the new market, and a sales force must be strong enough to convince consumers that you have what they want. This is no time for knee-jerk changes in management. Warner's Steve Ross felt impelled to hire a new executive, but management didn't make the video game market change. Managers need time to make the adjustments to a changed environment.

6

Product Failure
"Redesign It or Retire It"

THE EDSEL is synonymous with product failure. It was the most spectacular flop of its time. Ford's plan was to move out of its historic position as a producer of low-price cars into the lucrative midprice segment that GM had been dominating for decades. Not only were the late 1950s the time for Ford to make such a move, but, by using a basic Ford car as the framework for the product, it would yield an enormous profit margin. After all, how else could it push up the price on essentially the same product and attract the GM buyers without getting killed on tooling costs?

It didn't work, and the reason had little to do with the odd family name that Henry Ford II reluctantly agreed to use or the car's vertical oval grille. The failure was in Ford's penny-pinching design and poor quality. Furthermore, the Edsel was a transparency, not a new car. And it was launched in the midst of the 1958 recession, which further diminished it chances of success.

Earlier, another innovative car — the Chrysler Airflow — met a similar fate. An engineering triumph, replete with new features for the 1930s, including an aerodynamic all-steel body and four-wheel hydraulic brakes, the car flopped because consumers didn't appreciate its technical values. A few years later it probably would have been a smash hit.

Of course, there are plenty of products that are well timed for the market but fail because of engineering defects or uneconomical design. The first Reynolds ball point pen in the late 1940s is a classic example. It was a wonderful idea: no more messy ink or inkwells; no more blotters or fragile pen points to replace; gone forever the blue-splotched shirt pockets of the fountain pen era. Why, you could even write under water, as the ads said, or high in an airplane, as executives were doing more and more in those days.

The pens, though, didn't always live up to their billing. The ink flow was often erratic; on many occasions none came out. The joke was that the newfangled pens were the only kind of writing implement that could give you ten carbons with no original. Worse, the ink smeared under the heat of the human hand and seemed never to dry.

JEEP

At AMC, we found a failed product that was to become the lifeblood of the corporation for many years, once we refined it for use by the general public: the Jeep.

During World War II, the general purpose (GP) vehicle became known as the Jeep. It was the favorite of our troops. Ernie Pyle immortalized this roofless, indestructible transporter of two to four soldiers (usually officers and sergeants), and Bill Mauldin's cartoon of the distraught GI, his .45-caliber pistol thrust against the hood of his Jeep to end its misery, is one of the enduring images of the war. Americans loved the military Jeep to the point where it became a cult vehicle, and after the war there was a brisk business selling surplus Jeeps.

Years later, the Kaiser Corporation brought out a new model known as the CJ — the civilian Jeep. It was a far different vehicle from the austere military transport; it was heavier, plusher, and larger. But it still had much of the appeal of the original, and it also had the four-wheel drive that made it so useful off the road. Though it did not sell in large numbers, it developed a faithful following among those who had business away from the regular roadways. AMC looked at Jeep as a possible acquisition several times during the 1960s, but backed away each time, despite the warm relationship between our chairman and Kaiser's management.

In the 1970s, though, circumstances changed. Jeep had become a failure. It suffered from management neglect, and the buyer was beginning to catch on. Kaiser wanted to unload it.

Buying the company was simple. All we had to do was come up with $10 million in cash, $50 million more in AMC stock, and a note for the remaining $10 million. Even though I felt otherwise at the time, in retrospect I acknowledge that the purchase was one of the best bargains ever presented to a modern automobile company; the brand name alone was worth the price. AMC pulled Jeep out of its product crisis by redesigning almost every one of its parts: new engine, new transmission, Levi's trim, modern colors, and additional instruments. The vehicles have lasted and are still popular, but they would have been long gone by now if we had not carried out a major product overhaul. This was a good example of obvious product neglect overcome by dedicated management. Redesigned

Jeeps were supplied to a hungry market. It would have been criminal — and dumb — to let them die.

Why Products Fail

There are several reasons that products fail, the most common being that the engineers mess up the design or that the design does not satisfy the market.

But there is a third reason that is most troublesome and leads to some fearful crises. That is when the product design is workable and initially meets the need of the market but has latent flaws that become apparent only after the product has been in widespread use for a time. The worst frights are caused by products with flaws that endanger the health and safety of their users.

PROCTER & GAMBLE

An excellent example of such a product was Procter & Gamble's Rely brand of tampons. The product was based on two new fibers that increased its absorbency considerably over that of cotton, formerly the staple material of tampons. Rely was introduced in 1977 to immediate success; later, the bad news began to trickle in. By 1980, 890 cases of toxic shock syndrome had been reported to the Centers for Disease Control in Atlanta. At first no one made any connection between the disorder and the product; it was just another of those baffling mishaps. Then, an epidemiologist noticed that many of the victims were menstruating women. Following that clue, researchers soon found that a common element in many of the cases was the use of Rely tampons. P & G moved quickly to remove the product from the market.

Although the connection had been made, and the Cincinnati-based company had reacted swiftly, it was not until almost five years later, in 1985, that scientists learned that the new fibers acted to increase the growth of the toxic shock bacteria by absorbing magnesium from women's bodies.

P & G's alert response saved it from the pain of an unmanaged crisis. Indeed, it is hard to fault the company on any ground. The product was as well engineered as anyone could expect, given the state of the art at the time it was developed, and it was well received in the market. The initial evidence linking Rely to toxic shock was hardly damning. The company could have chosen to take a legalistic stance. Nothing had been proven; it was therefore obliged to do nothing. That is a common approach, and often a wrong one. By weighing the available information, and correctly concluding that there was a connection between Rely and toxic shock, P & G made the right moves. It must have been painful to pull from store shelves a product developed at considerable time and expense, but by doing so, the company avoided the horrendous costs of product liability suits that surely would have followed if it had kept the product on the market. Instead, P & G emerged as a company not afraid to incur loss in order to protect its customers.

The key to how a company will react to crisis caused by a latent product defect is the chief executive. If he is a leader, self-confident and secure, his reaction will be swift and responsible. The lawyers should get a hearing, of course, but the defense must not be evasive nor the company totally silent. "No comment" implies ignorance, indifference, and, most of all, guilt. The "spill the beans" public relations advisers should not prevail either, since there is no sense in making life easy for hostile trial lawyers. The prescription is to find out what is wrong, limit the damage, and see whether the product can be salvaged by redesign. If it cannot be fixed, abandon it.

A. H. ROBINS

It is instructive to contrast P & G's responsible action with the way the A. H. Robins Company mishandled the tragedies that arose from its Dalkon Shield contraceptive device. Robins, a 119-year-old pharmaceutical firm based in Richmond, Virginia, bought the rights to produce the plastic device, about the size of a nickel, from some private investors in 1970. The following year it sold the first of 4.5 million intrauterine devices, even though it had no gynecologists on its staff to check for possible side effects. Investigators believed that the string attached to the shield acted as a "wick," drawing infectious bacteria into the uterus, causing sickness and sometimes sterility. But the warnings were ignored by top management. The evidence of precrisis nonperformance of the product was denied again and again — a sure indication that trouble lay ahead.

Instead of reconsidering the product design, Robins aggressively marketed the shield for three years, despite evidence of infection, miscarriages, and, in a few instances, deaths associated with its use. In 1974 the evidence became overwhelming that the device was a health hazard, and the lawsuits began to mount. Robins first stopped promoting the product and finally, in early 1975, stopped its sale. The company termed its action a "market withdrawal" rather than a recall, because it had not been ordered by the Food and Drug Administration.

Management's attitude was an indication that it was suffering from too large an injection of legal advice. It maintained that the product was safe even after it had implicitly acknowledged its failings by stopping sales. "Our company has never viewed the Dalkon Shield as posing any risk higher than that associated with other IUDs," Robins's president declared in 1984. The company tried to manage its crisis by denying it, which is no management at all.

By refusing to recall the shields already in use, by following its lawyers' advice to avoid any appearance of liability, the company multiplied its problems. More women got sick; they lost children, their fertility, their lives. Then, in 1979, a federal court awarded $6.8 million to a Colorado woman who had miscarried and nearly died of infection while wearing a Dalkon Shield. The dam was broken; the stone wall had not worked. The defense strategy had failed, and the precrisis period was ending. Stunned, Robins began quietly advising doctors to remove the shields. Still the suits mounted, until over twelve thousand cases had been filed and over twenty deaths had been attributed to use of the device.

It was not until October 1984, over ten years after the product was withdrawn from the market, that Robins finally started a television and print campaign urging women wearing the Dalkon Shield to see their doctors and have it removed. The pressure on the company had become enormous: together with its insurers, it had settled seventy-six hundred suits for $245 million. But thousands more were still pending, and claims could have topped $1 billion. The company's effort to have the law changed to limit its liability had failed completely, and it had angered a federal judge, Miles W. Lord, with its court tactics of forcing women plaintiffs to reveal intimate details of their sexual activities. "I should have put them in jail," he said of Robins managers on the television program "60 Minutes." Denouncing the company for "monstrous mischief," he sent investigators rummaging through its files, where they turned up evidence that Robins had attempted to conceal its knowledge of the shield's dangers.

E. Claiborne Robins, Jr., the chief executive, grew desperate. In April 1985 the company set aside a reserve of $615 million to pay off the suits, by far the largest provision of its kind in the history of product liability cases. The $3.00 plastic implant had been costly indeed. But the reserve did not stem the tide of litigation. The poorly managed crisis was out of control, and its full weight was on Robins's managers. Finally, with no options other than financial ruin, Robins filed for protection under Chapter 11 of the bankruptcy laws on August 21, 1985. An unmanaged crisis had produced radical change.

P & G handled the Rely crisis, potentially as damaging as the Dalkon Shield crisis, by carefully assessing the evidence and then swiftly moving to limit the losses. At the same time, the company was acting ethically. Claiborne Robins dragged his feet and regarded the health effects of the product as factors in a strictly legal battle. Maybe he just hoped the problem would go away. In the end, the company was consumed by the crisis.

The following year, in March 1986, federal prosecutors accused management of illegal payments to officers and unauthorized payment of royalties. They sought to oust management, including Robins, and to turn control of the company over to a trustee appointed by the court. Meanwhile, the company said its general counsel, William A. Forest, Jr., would retire early, and it dismissed its outside bankruptcy lawyers for permitting improper payments.

SCHLITZ

Frank Sellinger knew the brewer's art. He may not have been the complete solution to the flagging fortunes of Joseph Schlitz Brewing Company when he arrived as president in 1977, but he was no stranger to the business.

Starting in the 1930s, he had worked as a chemist and marketing executive for a brewery — he even owned his own distribution company for a few years — and wound up as executive vice president of the dominant company in the beer industry, Anheuser-Busch. He knew how to make the product, transport it, market it, improve the flavor and appeal, and how to reduce the cost of production.

What was beyond his talents — and may have been beyond anyone's — was an ability to restructure a company that was in the final stages of a postcrisis decline. When Sellinger arrived at Schlitz, it was running out of time; he had precious few options to choose from, control was slipping out of his hands, and the problems of the company were growing even bigger. He piled up cash without a clear plan for using it. "We invested it nightly. I was getting as high as eighteen to twenty percent interest," boasted Sellinger. Because he had spent a lifetime in the operations end of the beer business, he was not prepared for a sudden switch in tactics by a much smaller but more maneuverable competitor he had sought to acquire. Sellinger ended up losing his company to soft-spoken, patrician Peter Stroh, the chief executive of the family-owned Stroh Brewery.

Schlitz was once the "beer that made Milwaukee famous," one of the two major premium beers in the country. The other, of course, was Anheuser-Busch's Budweiser. The beer business is built largely on illusion. Industry insiders say a premium beer is one that consumers are willing to pay more to drink; whether it actually has a better taste is a highly subjective evaluation. Industry legend has it that in the 1950s Anheuser-Busch had more brewing capacity than its home town St. Louis market could absorb, but couldn't expand its operation because shipping beer, which is mostly water, over long distances is expensive. An out-of-town beer would have to be priced higher than the local brew to make any money.

That's when A-B developed the concept of the premium beer. They said Bud was better than local suds and charged more for it. The gambit, reinforced by copious advertising, worked. Seventy percent of all the beer drunk in this country is consumed by 20 percent of the beer drinkers; these consumers, largely blue-collar workers, consider themselves experts on the subject of beer. They accepted Bud as the "king of beers" and willingly paid more for the privilege of moving upmarket.

Schlitz imitated the tactic and built a following across the nation, escaping its Milwaukee origins. Schlitz and Bud were the big national brands, with the hundreds of other breweries remaining largely local. These smaller brewers were mostly concerned about their home markets, and many were still owned by the descendants of the German families who had founded them back in the 1880s to supply a familiar product to their fellow immigrants.

Schlitz was owned by the Uihlein family, whose hundreds of members seemed to sit on the boards of all the charitable and cultural institutions in the Milwaukee area. Under the direction of Robert A. Uihlein, the fourth generation of his family to manage the company, Schlitz in the 1970s set as its goal low-cost production. This is standard business school doctrine; a low-cost producer will eventually become dominant in a commodity market. But buying beer is not a wholly rational decision; since actual differences in taste are so slight, it is the illusion of quality that is paramount.

Sensitive to its hold on beer drinkers' illusions, A-B stuck with its traditional brewing process, though scientific advances would have enabled it to produce a comparable product more quickly and cheaply. Schlitz chose to go the other way. In the early 1970s it started substituting corn syrup for rice and other grains in the brewing process. Then it cut back on the use of barley malt, a relatively expensive ingredient that gives beer flavor and body. Company executives boasted about how they had "changed" their beer, emphasizing that they had cut their costs in an effort to boost the price of Schlitz stock. Finally, Schlitz switched to something called "accelerated batch fermentation," which involves the injection of air into the brew, cutting the aging time by 35 to 40 percent.

The financial results were impressive at first. In 1973, even though Schlitz lagged well behind A-B in sales, it earned 21 percent on stockholders' equity, compared with 13.8 percent for the larger company. With greater productivity and lower-cost materials, it was able to earn 7.6 percent on sales, compared with Anheuser-Busch's 5.9 percent. But the numbers, cherished as they are by financial analysts, told only part of the story. Experts argued that the changes cut costs without materially affecting the product — but damage had been done to the illusion. With a good deal of help from Schlitz's competitors, serious beer drinkers began to take the view that Schlitz beer had been "changed" for the worse and "cheapened." It was now considered inferior to the beers produced by longer, more costly processes.

Schlitz executives were defensive. "In the brewing business," one complained, "if you say you use the same process your ancestors used to make beer in 1700, people think that's good; but if you use the same transportation your ancestors used in 1700, people question your sanity." Troubles compounded. At one stockholders' meeting a disaffected member of the Uihlein family stood up and waved a bottle of cloudy beer, the result of a production mistake that had resulted in flakes precipitating out of solution.

The product was failing, the reaction was swift, and the

crisis deepened. Schlitz's growth peaked in 1976, with production of twenty-four million barrels of beer, but by 1980 it had fallen to fifteen million barrels. Meanwhile, Philip Morris, the cigarette company, had bought Miller Brewing Company and, by applying modern advertising and marketing techniques, had promoted it to the status of a national, premium beer. Schlitz, once the second largest brand in the nation, fell behind Miller and seemed on an irreversible downward slide. Desperate managers decided tough advertising was the answer: "Go for the gusto" ads were replaced by glowering former boxers who snarled, "You want to take away my gusto?" The ads were dubbed "Drink my Schlitz or I'll kill you" in the industry and were pulled off the air after about a year.

With their crisis marching into its final stages, Schlitz's board reached out for Sellinger, then at Anheuser-Busch. It was a big shift for the burly executive, who was known for his attention to operating detail and love of a good scrap. He would be leaving the industry leader for a company that was clearly struggling, but he could be the top man, something not possible at A-B as long as the Busch family retained control. Sellinger was appointed president of Schlitz in late 1977 and immediately set about reformulating the beer, adding barley malt and slowing down the aging process. The company's competitors acknowledged the improvement, but former consumers didn't seem to care.

In a daring move, Schlitz commissioned live television advertisements, managed by football referee Tommy Bell, showing beer drinkers comparing unmarked samples of Schlitz with Budweiser and Miller. Naturally, the results were favorable, but the market remained unmoved. When there is little real difference between products, the shattering of an illusion is fatal. Sellinger himself said there are no instances of a beer brand's recovering once its sales slip by over 30 percent. By 1979, Schlitz had fallen deeply into the red, losing $50.6 million. The need for radical change was now widely accepted.

Sellinger, seeking merger partners, approached the big soft drink and food companies. They were not interested, and antitrust laws prevented his striking a deal with Anheuser-Busch or Miller. Sellinger rejected an advance by Peter Stroh to buy Schlitz with the nonpublic Stroh stock, and a proposed deal with Heileman, another midsize brewing company, was turned down by federal authorities, at least partly because of complaints by Stroh. Sellinger said he felt safe in accumulating cash, because no one seemed interested in taking over Schlitz; he would use the funds to try once again to establish the fading brand in the market. Then came a shock.

"The Monday before Good Friday in 1982, I got a call from Peter Stroh again, suggesting that Schlitz buy Stroh's," Sellinger said. "Well, I couldn't get there fast enough." Since Stroh's was privately held — it still is — accountants spent the week going over the books to ascertain what kinds of assets and liabilities Schlitz would be acquiring. Sellinger felt confident enough to leave the following weekend to go to Phoenix to meet with an auto-racing team Schlitz was sponsoring. But Peter Stroh, a quiet, unassuming, and pleasant man who had worked for the Central Intelligence Agency in the 1950s before a traffic accident ended his career there, was readying a surprise counterthrust.

"I got a call from our public relations department on Sunday," Sellinger recalled, "saying 'Frank, a friend in the composing room of *The Wall Street Journal* says there is a tombstone ad in tomorrow's paper saying that Stroh's is going to tender for you.'" It was an audacious move. Schlitz was several times the size of Stroh's in terms of sales and was long established nationally; because he had a family-owned company, Peter Stroh was literally betting the homestead on the outcome. "Later that evening I got hold of Peter, whom I had known since my days as a wholesaler in the Columbus, Ohio, area," Sellinger remembered. "I said, 'Is it true that you're going to tender for us?' He said, 'Yes, we changed our minds.'"

While the negotiations were under way for the ostensible sale of Stroh's to Schlitz, Peter Stroh had quietly lined up loans totaling $310 million to attempt a takeover of Schlitz. Sellinger resisted, and succeeded in boosting the price from $15 a share to $17, but the game was over. No reasonable defense could be mounted; too many members of the Uihlein family had sold their stock to Wall Street's arbitrageurs. Asked if he was still in touch with Peter Stroh, a man he had known since he was twenty-one years old, Sellinger smiles. "I don't think you would say we are the greatest of friends. Never did we think Strohs would tender for us."

Once it had control of Schlitz, Stroh's moved quickly to close the Milwaukee headquarters and dismiss most of Schlitz's management. The product failed in the early 1970s; a decade later the company disappeared. Stroh's got what it wanted, a nationwide system of modern, efficient breweries and a network of distributors. It added Schlitz's very successful Old Milwaukee popular-price brand and some others to its market line-up. But new ownership hasn't helped the Schlitz brand, which continues to wither in the market.

COCA-COLA

Schlitz's product failure was the inadvertent result of a misplaced concentration on the wrong goals; the Coca-Cola Company plunged into disaster with its eyes wide open. Here again the differences between the product involved and its major rivals were small and hard to measure. People know they "like" a brand of soft drink based on a mixture of taste and promotion. "Coke is it," say the slogans, but what is "it"? As Coke discovered to its dismay, whatever constitutes "it" ran far more deeply in people's consciousness than the company had imagined.

Coke's chairman, a chemical engineer named Roberto Goizueta, had been concerned that the company's flagship soft drink, the ninety-nine-year-old Coca-Cola, was losing market share to Pepsi-Cola. Pepsi, somewhat sweeter and less fizzy, was attracting large numbers of younger buyers, who didn't like the slight burning sensation Coke left in the back of their throats. The company began tinkering with the secret formula that had been so closely guarded for a century, trying to come up with a product that would enable it to regain lost ground. Unlike Schlitz, it wasn't trying to cut costs; Goizueta wanted to be sure the company was being firmly managed, that a mindless attachment to the past was not going to be allowed to permit market share to slip away.

Everything was carefully planned. Patrick Caddell, whose polls had helped promote Jimmy Carter to the presidency, was hired to test public reaction to a new Coke formula. For over four years, people were asked to taste test samples of unmarked soft drinks. Over 190,000 people were tested, and the majority said they preferred the sweeter version. It was all there in the reports, columns of numbers giving in precise detail the results of the most scientific taking of the public's pulse that money could buy.

So Goizueta decided on a dramatic gesture. He would skip the test marketing that is usually carried out to check public acceptance of a new product. After all, he had just launched Diet Coke without market testing and it was a smash success. Confidence was high, as it often is before a crisis strikes — but the basic assumptions that go untested can undo the best plan.

The market research in the blind tests gave plenty of evidence of changing public taste. And competitors would soon hear of any attempt to test a reformulated Coke; they would be quick to seize on any uncertainty over Coke's confidence in its flagship brand. No, it was decided, the way to go was to scrap the old Coke and introduce the new formula. In April 1985, to a blare of self-generated publicity, Coke put into a bank vault in Atlanta the formula that had made it an institution around the world and introduced the new Coke. For a while the bold stroke seemed to work. Private company polls in May showed reaction to the new Coke was favored 53 to 47 percent.

But the pre-introduction polls had not told the people being tested that their preference for the new formula meant the Coke they had grown up with would be scrapped. Who knows what the results would have been if the issue was framed as it was to be in the real world. Decades of advertising, weaving Coke into the fabric of American life, prompted a stunning backlash. Coke as it had been known was associated with good times, old sweethearts, sporting events, and all the other things concomitant with the American way. By taking it away, a big company was cuffing around millions of Americans, and they resented it. Sentiment began to change. By early July, the company's polls showed that the new brand's approval rating had fallen to 30 percent.

Coke's initial reaction was to leave the crisis unmanaged. Just hang on, it told its distributors. The new formula will take hold. Hadn't the pre-introduction surveys showed that people really preferred the sweeter drink? This nonperformance, in not properly presenting the choice to test subjects, was followed by denial. We can't be wrong, Coke executives said; we have the data. There probably was nothing wrong with the product. What failed was how it fitted into the market. The new Coke was pre-emptive; it was substituted for something that had been around for decades and had acquired a momentum of its own. Consumers formed groups demanding the old Coke, and others hoarded cases of the familiar product. Songs were written imploring the company to "just give us back the taste of Coke." The media loved the controversy and helped fan the flames of resentment.

The company tried to tough it out, but the bottlers, independent businessmen who control Coke's distribution, demanded action. Coke, they said, was in danger of slipping behind Pepsi-Cola because of the furor. By July, just a few months after the new Coke was introduced, but before the crisis slipped completely out of control, the company threw in the towel. The new formula would remain, but the old Coke would be revived, they said, as Coke Classic. The decision was made quickly, without any detailed advertising or marketing plans in place, based on the outcry from the bottlers and the "gut feeling" on the part of many Coke executives that the market was slipping away. It took a cool head at the top — a man confident enough to swallow a mistake — to act this deliberately under fire. Roberto Goizueta looked reality in the eye and reversed himself. Some cynics said Coke had planned on having two versions all along, and that killing off the old Coke was a ploy to attract attention to the brand. Company insiders say there was no such scheme and that the incident was too damaging to have been brought on voluntarily. "It's been a humbling experience," said Donald R. Keough, the president of Coca-Cola.

Coke's managers were arrogant in setting aside the product that had been carrying the company for almost a century before they had tested its replacement in the marketplace. They had no plan to deal with failure; all systems were geared to promote the "new" Coke, because management believed that if they pressed hard enough, it would be a success. When the market flinched, they hesitated to take action, hoping things would turn around. But to their credit, when it became quite clear that they goofed, they moved quickly. Having failed in their objective of transferring Coke's heritage to the new product, they brought back the old one.

They dealt with an incipient product failure by getting in touch with their customers, identifying the problem, and responding rapidly. If they had hesitated, they might well have found themselves in the same straits as Schlitz or Robins. Coke was not prepared for a crisis, but Goizueta and his staff kept their antennae up, a vital aspect of good crisis management. The trick is to sense trouble early and act on clear evidence, even if it is incomplete. In the end, Coke managed things reasonably well; the ability to react with courage and speed when failure is detected is what makes heroes out of crisis managers.

7

Top Management Succession
"Weakness at the Top"

As DIFFICULT as it sometimes is to get the right chief executive into office, it can be even harder to get him out. It may be perfectly obvious to the board, creditors, employees, customers, and even shareholders that the Old Man should quit — the only one who can't see it is the CEO himself. Too often, though, the board doesn't have the guts to stand up to the man who gave them their power in the first place.

Zbigniew Brzezinski, the national security adviser to President Jimmy Carter, noted that the smartest political leader, on attaining high office, proceeds to eliminate those who put him there. Many CEOs have found this to be the road to longevity; once a chief executive has packed his board with cheerleaders, they are not likely to be eager to act as pallbearers.

Bill Agee worked this trick at Bendix before staging his disastrous attack on Martin Marietta. He pushed out directors whose support he could not be sure of, finding conflicts of interest that had not seemed to matter before he took over. With a compliant board, he felt bold enough to launch his ill-fated assault, and to stay in the fray, even though the two corporations were on the verge of devouring each other with possibly catastrophic consequences. When the board members could stand it no longer, they didn't unseat Agee — they just took to the lifeboats and resigned. Agee has since said of the defections, "That was the first time I felt my crisis getting out of control." Had the board been in control, the outcome might have been different.

OCCIDENTAL PETROLEUM

At eighty-six, Armand Hammer, the chairman of the $20-billion-a-year Occidental Petroleum Corporation, is a man of great vitality and prominence. He travels the world, meeting with heads of state and putting together gargantuan deals. Still, he and the company have a problem. Who will succeed him? Time after time he has groomed a successor, only to feel hot breath on his neck. In each case, he found fault with the chosen one, who in short order was dismissed and another disposable favorite installed. *Business Week* described Hammer as "the beneficiary of the ultimate executive perk: he gets to operate the company as if it were his private fiefdom." Hammer controls the board because of his personal reputation — he is one of the few foreigners permitted to fly a corporate jet through Soviet airspace — and because he casts out those who would challenge him.

When David Murdock, a wealthy entrepreneur who sat on Occidental's board, disagreed with Hammer's strategy and considered a takeover battle, Hammer had the company buy Murdock's 5 percent stockholding for a $53 million premium over market price. When Murdock's stock was gone, so was his board seat. Robert Abboud, a blunt-spoken former banker, was dismissed in 1984, after four years as president, for daring to dissent from the views of "the Doctor," as Hammer is called, in deference to the medical degree he earned many years ago. Abboud was the sixth president Hammer had forced out in sixteen years.

In spite of his age, Hammer continues to commit the company to long-term deals that may take years to pay off (if they ever do) because of his belief that oil will one day fetch $100 a barrel. Disregarding his advanced years, he has flatly refused to designate a successor. Instead, he has arranged for a contract that will keep him in office until 1989, with automatic yearly renewals after that. Unable to accept the thought of retirement, he has created a potential vacuum at the top and has put Occidental in a precrisis state. The crisis will erupt on the day he dies or is disabled, but Occidental's board does not seem inclined to take any action to prevent its happening.

AMC

The top management succession that moved me up from executive vice president to CEO at American Motors was peculiar but instructive, and I was certainly pleased with the result. It began one winter afternoon in 1975, when I was summoned to Roy Chapin's office. As I walked past the big oak door into the chairman's office, Roy pushed a button under his desk that made the door swing silently closed. Once inside, I realized that we were not alone; with Roy was our president, Bill Luneberg, and our vice president for marketing, Bill McNealy.

Luneberg was a character. He kept a big rubber stamp on his desk so that he could slam "Bullshit" in red on any document he didn't like. He was well remembered by officials of the Chase Manhattan Bank for his antics in the midst of a credit renegotiation during one of AMC's tough periods. When the talks got rough, he blew up and shouted, "If you guys keep this up, you're going to own an automobile company." Then he pulled the keys to his office from his pocket, threw them across the table at the startled bankers, and stormed out of the room. It was all an act, but it was typical of him.

Roy Chapin was Luneberg's antithesis. As rough, fun-loving and boisterous as Luneberg was, Chapin is the quiet gentleman. Cultured and urbane, he has a manner that bespeaks "old money," and he lives a life appropriate to a scion of Grosse Point. Never uttering a blue word, always the diplomat, gentle almost to a fault, he is easy to like.

Chapin did the talking. "Bill and I have been doing some thinking about management succession. We will be around for a while, of course, but we have concluded that it is time to designate successors now so that you can prepare yourselves for what's coming." He looked at Bill McNealy and said, "You and Gerry will be the replacements for Bill and me in the positions of chairman and president. We have decided not to indicate which of you will take which spot, preferring to decide and announce that later."

It was the beginning of a bad time — actually a pre-crisis period — for me and the company. We were to be racked by a divisiveness that didn't heal for years. Word about the meeting leaked out almost immediately, and within a month it became necessary to acknowledge that the succession decision had been partially made. That only made things worse. Everybody took sides, and it was difficult for us on top to discourage it. McNealy and I carefully refrained from open hostilities, but alone with our people each of us moved with a vengeance to look good at our adversary's expense. We learned at first hand how destructive it is to an organization to select multiple heirs apparent, the winner to be decided later.

This approach doesn't make much sense when you think about it, yet it is often followed. Long before his retirement, Walter Wriston, the chairman of Citicorp, identified three candidates for his job — John Reed, Thomas Theobald, and Hans Angermuller. In the end, Reed got the job and the other two were publicly humiliated. A year later, in September 1985, in an effort to draw on the energy of one of the losers, Reed put Theobald in charge of the bank's increasingly important investment banking activities.

Reginald Jones at General Electric tapped four potential heirs to his CEO throne — Stanley C. Gault, John F. Welch, Robert Frederick, and Thomas Vanderslice. He chose Welch, and the others left. Edwin D. Dodd at Owens-Illinois designated Robert Lanigan and William Spangler as front runners as his successor. When the tussle was over, the loser, Spangler, found that there was no place left for him in the company. Chief executives employ this tactic to show how great is the power they wield and how difficult it is for anyone else to attain their status. In fact, the gambit diminishes their stature, bringing embarrassment to the company and causing it to lose the talents of some of its best people.

At AMC the competition and infighting went on until the fall of 1978 — three long years. In June 1977, Luneberg resigned and I was elected president and chief operating officer. McNealy was chosen as vice chairman. But the race had not ended, since the board was still split over who would be the next chief executive. They decided on an executive "shoot-out." McNealy and I were each asked to prepare a plan for the corporation and have it ready for the November 1977 board meeting. It was clear that the more convincing presentation would win. (By this time, John DeLorean had come and gone as a contender.)

The day arrived, and McNealy went on first. His plan, in essence, was to drop the car business and concentrate on Jeep. I said that we needed both cars and Jeeps, and that I would attempt to save the car business. We were closely questioned, as we should have been: the most important decisions a board of directors makes are who will be the corporation's chief executive and where the company should be going. In this case, AMC's directors ended the succession crisis, rose to the occasion, as I like to describe it, and selected me.

On November 15, 1977, I was elected chief executive of American Motors; a year later I gained the chairman's title. McNealy resigned. It need not have happened that way — I would have been glad to keep him in a senior capacity — but the price of grooming multiple successors is that you lose the losers.

UNITED TECHNOLOGIES

Harry J. Gray has a lot in common with Armand Hammer. Both have taken companies from relative insignificance to great dimensions; both have worked very hard all their lives; both have identified themselves closely with their companies (Hammer holds annual meetings on his birthday); both can legitimately claim that the success of their companies is due to their individual leadership and vision; both dominate their boards. Gray is nearing the point where his tenure at the top would end under ordinary circumstances; Hammer has long passed that point. Neither, however, shows any eagerness to depart. Both have managed to ease out heirs apparent before they become real threats. Hammer has not named a viable successor or developed a visible plan of succession; Gray was finally forced into one. Neither is poor or dependent on his current earnings to maintain his style of living, but neither would know how to handle retirement.

The succession crisis is a corporate disease that afflicts successful and self-made leaders. It is fairly common in small and moderate-size companies, particularly those that are privately owned, and occurs most often in family companies. But large, publicly owned companies can suffer from this disease as well. United Technologies is one of them.

Harry Gray did not found United Technologies; the company dates back to 1929 and at one time owned both the Boeing Aircraft Company and United Airlines. Indeed, Gray seemed headed in directions other than business early in his career, when he earned bachelor's and master's degrees in journalism. But after a brief period of teaching English, he moved into business and by 1969 was senior executive vice president of Litton Industries. Blocked from advancement there by the presence of the founders, Charles (Tex) Thornton and Roy Ash, he moved to what was then United Aircraft, a respected but somewhat stodgy producer of Pratt & Whitney jet engines and Sikorsky helicopters.

He reshaped the company to match his vision, acquiring high-technology companies and changing the corporation's name to reflect its new composition. Under his management, sales grew from about $2 billion in 1971 to $16 billion in 1984, and earnings rose from a loss of $44 million in 1971 to a profit of $620 million in 1984. Unquestionably, Gray, an exceedingly talented and capable executive of considerable charm, had taken the company and formed it into his own instrument. He also made clear by his actions that he was not eager to put it down.

The UT board began pestering him in the mid 1970s to lay out a clear path of succession following his mandatory retirement at the age of sixty-five. But Gray evidences a low regard for the effectiveness of boards of directors. He told my business school class in 1986 that boards "can ooh and aah and grunt and disapprove, but they can't really do much other than hire and fire the chief executive officer." Appearing to yield to the pressure for a line of succession, Gray began a series of maneuvers that seemed to provide for his replacement, but these somehow always wound up with him in firm control.

Edward Hennessy was the first heir apparent. Arriving from Heublein in 1972, he performed well as a financial analyst and planner, and his responsibilities were broadened. Gray held the titles of president, chairman, and chief executive officer, but when the board suggested making Hennessy president in 1978, Gray balked. Executive vice president was as high as Hennessy was going to rise as long as Gray was in charge. Hennessy got the message and left the following year to run the Allied Corporation.

Next, Gray tried what one former director terms "the Haig gambit." Alexander Haig, the former adviser to presidents, four-star general, and retired commander of NATO, was available. For a company that sold one fourth of its annual output to the military, Haig's attraction was obvious. Though he had had no corporate management experience — which to Gray may have seemed an asset rather than a liability — Haig was made president and chief operating officer in December 1979. For the first time, Gray appeared to have yielded some of his power. The appearance was greater than the reality. Shortly after arriving, Haig underwent a triple by-pass heart operation. Then, barely a year after arriving, he resigned to become secretary of state in the new Reagan administration. Gray was once again alone at the top.

Gray was then sixty-one years old, and the board was pressing harder for a succession plan, fearing a vacuum if something should happen to Gray. He responded by setting up a horse race between two of the company's most promising executives, Peter Scott, the head of the electronics group, and Robert Carlson, who was running the Pratt & Whitney operation. One was to be the successor; neither made it.

The shoot-out approach to determining top management had its usual destructive effects, and in 1983 Scott dropped out, saying that he preferred to be an entrepreneur. At the time this happened, I called Harry and asked him why Scott had left. He shot back: "He just walked in one day and said 'I quit.' What else could I do but go over to Carlson and congratulate him?" Carlson did seem to be the winner, and he was given the title of president. He was not made chief operating officer, though, and large sections of the company reported not to him, but directly to Gray.

As Gray's sixty-fifth birthday approached, he began to find fault with Carlson. The board rejected a four-year extension of Gray's term — until 1989 — but did go along with a one-year extension until the end of 1985. A month before Carlson was to become chief executive officer, Gray launched a bitter attack on him at the September 1984 board meeting.

Since then Gray has refused to discuss the incident, saying only "he just didn't perform and that was the end of it." Carlson resigned, but not before countercharging that Gray had bugged his home in an effort to find something incriminating. A special panel of the board was named to investigate the charges, and though Gray was cleared, pressure mounted to restore the appearance of order. The following month Robert Daniell, who had been with the Sikorsky helicopter subsidiary for most of his career, was named president and chief operating officer. Some questioned whether Daniell had a broad enough background for the job; Carlson, they noted, was a much stronger candidate. A top airline executive told *Business Week* that Daniell's rise was "a classic case of the second-best guy getting a lucky break."

Finally, in September 1985, a year after forcing out Carlson, Gray agreed to relinquish the chief executive's title to Daniell on January 1, 1986. Significantly, though, he held on as chairman and gave no indication that he was about to quit the scene. Gray would stay on "at the discretion of the board," the company said. Some analysts think that despite Daniell's fast start Gray is still in control, that the succession issue is by no means settled, that a crisis at the top is still a definite prospect. UT was mentioned as a takeover target during the Gray-Carlson battle, and it could become one again if Gray starts maneuvering once more to hold on to the power he so obviously enjoys.

LEHMAN BROTHERS

I did not know Pete Peterson all that well, but we were close enough that I called and suggested that we have lunch in early 1982. When I arrived at his offices at 55 Water Street, all seemed calm and controlled. I had no idea that Peterson was involved in a cut-and-thrust battle for power with Lew Glucksman, a man he had promoted many times and thought he had come to terms with.

Without knowing it, I was seated in the midst of the biggest private management succession crisis in Wall Street history. An unmanaged crisis flashed into the open soon enough, though, with the predictable result: radical change.

Lehman Brothers was one of the pillars of Wall Street; 134 years old, the longest continuing investment banking partnership in the nation's financial capital, it had its own way of life. As *The New York Times* put it, "Handshakes as solid as contracts . . . loyalty between a bank and a client . . . fierce but respectful competition . . . a belief in the firm as something larger than self." But it was brought down by an unresolvable power struggle at the top. As one partner said afterward, "This is a firm that survived the Civil War between the North and South, and could not survive the civil war between Peterson and Glucksman."

I had come to know Peterson as a result of some work Lehman had done in connection with AMC's merger with Renault, and he had always been pleasant and helpful. After I left AMC, he was the logical person to see as I worked my network of contacts to find opportunities. We dined alone. The arrangement of the bone china place settings made it clear that one of us was going to enjoy the view of the southern tip of Manhattan and the Statue of Liberty and the other was to face a wall. Pete took the seat with the view and waved for me to sit across from him. After welcoming me warmly, he launched into a discussion of French politics and French business meetings, and startled me with a rather long discourse on the arrogance of the French. At first, I thought he was trying to ingratiate himself after hearing about some of the disagreements I had encountered in Paris. Then he cited several of his experiences in Washington with French counterparts when he was President Nixon's assistant for international affairs and later secretary of commerce. It struck me as strange that he didn't once mention Lehman Brothers or its business. He spent the entire discussion on the outside world, where his interests obviously lay. I had heard that Pete was "Mr. Outside," but now I became convinced that it was to the exclusion of everything inside. This was the weakness that felled him.

As we were talking, Mr. Inside, Lew Glucksman, was preparing to push Pete Peterson completely outside. Management succession was arising as a critical issue, threatening the future of the Lehman partnership — as it had several times before. For forty-four years before his death in 1969, Robert (Bobbie) Lehman, one of the grandsons of the founders, had led the firm. There were divisions and opposing camps during his years, but Bobbie was always able to pull things together. He left no plan for succession, though, and his death was followed by a period of chaos that insiders described as "the War of Roses."

Shortly after Lehman's death Frederick L. Ehrman had been installed as chairman, but he was an unpopular choice whose management style grated on the senior partners. Men who had successfully put together deals worth hundreds of millions of dollars did not relish being told that one of their proposals was "the stupidest idea I've ever heard," a favorite Ehrman line. The senior partners organized a palace revolution and toppled Ehrman. Needing a strong administrative hand at the helm, they turned to a man who had joined Lehman just two months earlier, in June 1973, and who had formerly been the chief executive of Bell & Howell as well as a high government official — Pete Peterson.

Ten years later, Peterson felt he had a succession plan of his own. He would stay on a few more years, until he was sixty, and then turn the company over to Glucksman. But he had lost touch with the details of the business and did not reckon on the smoldering resentments and ambitions of Glucksman, who had taken over day-to-day control of Lehman's operations.

Peterson had every reason to expect loyalty from Glucksman. After all, wasn't it he who had saved Glucksman's neck in 1973 when a collapse in the bond market had piled up huge losses for the firm? Though they were something of an odd couple, Peterson and Glucksman seemed to work well. Lehman had been reporting record earnings for the past five years; the money machine was humming and prospects were bright.

But Glucksman resented Peterson's getting all the glory while he dealt with the gritty details that produced the results. He felt the chairman treated him cavalierly, dropping big names from his days in government. And he let it be known that he wanted recognition. Peterson responded by making Glucksman co-chief executive in May 1983. Within a few months Glucksman demanded the top job exclusively for himself; Peterson would have to go. The partners, many of whom found the aggressive Glucksman too "pushy," were deeply split. Facing an internal uproar, Peterson agreed to step aside for a multimillion-dollar "golden handshake." The final parting was brutal. At a general partnership meeting Peterson explained why he was stepping aside. As he finished, Glucksman stood and dismissed him, saying, "Would you now leave and let me be with my partners."

Glucksman tried to impose stability, but many of the firm's key people resented what they saw as his raw lust for power. A product of the trading department, he favored traders over investment bankers, further irritating the open wounds at Lehman. Partners began to depart, taking customers with them. Although capital had never seemed to be a problem before, some partners began worrying openly that the firm's $176 million capital base was inadequate. By the fall of 1984, the vultures had begun to circle. Glucksman ignored one takeover bid and then made a classic managerial error: he permitted the board to meet without him. The leaderless board decided that selling the firm would allow all the partners to pull out their investments — and rid them of Glucksman's rule. Though they tried to act quietly, the press got word of the dissension and the firm became almost paralyzed. Near collapse at the height of the crisis, Lehman Brothers announced on April 10, 1984, that it would merge with the American Express Company, ending its almost century and a half as a private partnership. The partners made lots of money, but Lew Glucksman lost what he had really wanted — to be chief executive of a top Wall Street investment banking firm. A management succession crisis had destroyed an institution.

Partnerships are particularly vulnerable to problems of management succession; they have fuzzy lines of authority and are top-heavy with more-or-less equals. A partnership is a fragile device dependent on good relations between the partners and the leadership of the few selected to handle the executive functions. As an institution, it is poorly designed for management succession — secret agendas are commonplace. Since partnerships are private, most of the management succession struggles and crises rage on unseen, but the Lehman case was too big to hide. We got a good look at how an unmanaged crisis led to radical change.

8

Cash Crises
"Frequent and Lethal"

A CASH CRISIS is not a fundamental problem. Rather, it is a sign that something else has gone wrong. Nevertheless, it is among the most common of the serious difficulties that executives face and if not resolved will cause a business to fail.

I feel like an expert on the subject. In my twenty-one years at AMC, there were only two periods when I felt comfortable with the amount of cash we had on hand, and both were fleeting. One was when Jeep sales were booming in late 1978 and the other was a year later, just after Renault had taken an equity position in the company, injecting $150 million in cash by buying 22 percent of our common stock.

For years we counted cash by the greenback at AMC's headquarters in Southfield, Michigan. Often, we were down to a zero cash balance and on more occasions than I care to remember were actually into negative numbers. For a short while, though, we were flush, particularly in early 1978, when car sales were hot and trucks — which include Jeeps — were even hotter. Jeep sales had grown from 33,000 a year when we bought the company to an annual rate of 180,000. Fuel prices had been held down by government actions, and many people were using the four-wheel-drive Jeeps to travel off-road for fun. We had two plants running flat out producing Jeep vehicles and were readying two more to meet the seemingly limitless demand. A year later gasoline prices skyrocketed, and for the second time in a decade it became wrong to drive a gas guzzler. Jeeps were thirsty, and the off-road phenomenon died, not to revive until the mid 1980s.

Our cash flow dried up with Jeep sales; money became so short that we couldn't carry out our product plans. Worse, we were headed for default on our loan agreements unless we could get some help from Renault. We got it, but at the price of our sovereignty. It was hardball all the way; Renault's price was slightly more than 46 percent of our common stock and some convertible preferred. From then on, AMC was to be a Renault affiliate. I had no quarrel with this; Renault had bought control of the company fair and square. We did it to ensure a future for everybody involved.

CHRYSLER

Much earlier in my career, I was at Chrysler when it ran into a cash crunch in 1954 as the national economy slumped after the Korean War. Chrysler was in transition at the time. Lester (Tex) Colbert, who had a background in the law, had taken command from K. T. Keller, who had left the company stuck with products that were antiquated in appearance. In addition to facing a weakening market with outmoded products, Colbert had inherited crumbling factories and a shrinking market share.

He knew something had to be done, and lacking a strong vision of his own, Colbert looked ouside for assistance. He found McKinsey & Company, a management consulting firm that studied Chrysler and decided that the company was poorly organized and had loose financial controls.

Then Lynn Townsend, from Chrysler's public accounting firm Touche Ross Bailey & Smart, took charge. Townsend had a plan for the company that proved profitable at first, but foundered in later years. He tried to make Chrysler into a global company like General Motors and Ford, but wound up buying most of the failing car companies of Europe. Rather than strengthening Chrysler, the acquisitions sapped the resources of the parent company until it too became ill.

John Riccardo, Townsend's protégé at Touche Ross, took over next and was regarded as a shrewd financial manager. He would periodically visit me in Geneva, where I was director of financial analysis for Chrysler's overseas investments. Invariably, he opened with the question "What have we got in reserves?" He knew very well that we tried to smooth out profit fluctuations by having as much as possible in reserve accounts. If he could flush them out, he would have real profits to report back to Highland Park, where they were badly needed. But all his attention to finances did not prevent Chrysler from falling into a cash crisis that led the board to oust him in favor of Lee Iacocca.

So much has been written, by others and me earlier, about Chrysler — its long downward spiral, the struggle for federal loan guarantees, and the great Iacocca revival — that I hesitate to mention it again. But Chrysler's problem, from 1979 to 1982, was the archetype of the cash crisis in American industry. Seldom has so large a company faced so certain an end.

Of course, Chrysler had more than a cash crisis. It had — all at the same time — bad product, marketing, regulatory, public perception, and other crises. But in 1980 it all came down to cash. The company had hardly any and it needed plenty — on the order of $2 billion — right away to develop new products. It seemed impossible. The company wasn't making enough sales to earn the cash, and the lending institutions were too worried about the credits they had already extended to lend any more. Even a merger seemed out of the question: nobody wanted to make love to the old lady who had no virtue and had lost her looks too.

In fact, notwithstanding the efforts of Riccardo and his feisty president, Gene Cafiero, Chrysler was manifesting all the symptoms of an unmanaged crisis. The elements are clearly identifiable:

Chronic nonperformance. Everywhere.

Denial and recrimination. Management said everything was O.K.; they knew how to run the business. This line was replaced by the refrain that the government was to blame and they deserved help.

Anger and fear. The board realized that Chrysler could not make it without new management, and hired Iacocca.

In a case like this, what usually follows is the most critical phase: financial *failure* as the cash runs out, *panic,* and *collapse.* Even after Iacocca joined Chrysler, on November 2, 1978, the decline continued. It was not until June 10, 1980, that the company obtained approval of its loan guarantees from Washington. A few days later Chrysler drew down $500 million, giving it some breathing room. But every dollar was spoken for and more would be needed — $1.2 billion altogether.

The plea for federal aid was distasteful to all involved.

Steve Miller, then the company's controller, told me, "Frankly, the day I came to Chrysler I thought there has got to be some way to work this out without getting the government involved. It only took me about twenty-four hours to be disabused of that." The alternative to government assistance was bankruptcy — and that, he said, would have destroyed the company's network of dealers and made a comeback impossible.

A new top manager could not have been expected to save Chrysler on day one. It takes time to put together a crisis management team. In fact, Iacocca has since admitted that he didn't know how big a mess he was getting into. "If I had the slightest idea of what lay ahead for me when I joined Chrysler, I wouldn't have gone there for all the money in the world," he has said. It is an ironic statement, because the people he managed to hire during Chrysler's darkest days say it was because of their confidence in Iacocca and their belief in what he said could be done with the company that encouraged them to make the risky change. Steve Miller, now vice chairman, told my class, "I went to Chrysler from a comfortable job at Ford's Venezuela operation because I believed in Iacocca. I assumed he knew what he was into."

Shortly after the first federal loan draw-down, the automobile market swooned again, with interest rates shooting up and sales falling off. Chrysler was once more gasping for cash. "We got our cash level down to between $1 million and $10 million a day for a period of about three months," recalled Miller, whose major job at the time was scraping together operating funds. This was at a company that spent $50 million a day on average. Iacocca pulled together the top eight officers of the company and told each to squeeze more cash out of his operation. Nothing was to be overlooked; every cash source was to be identified and exploited.

The sales force was told to twist dealers' arms to order more cars to support an aggressive production schedule, though dealer lots were clogged with unsold inventory. The manufacturing people had to launch two new lines of cars, with no slip-ups. "We were in a position where the loss of half a day's production would put us out of business," Miller said. The finance department worked with the Federal Reserve System to speed up delivery of cash from dealers, which produced $30 million. A deal with the Export-Import Bank to finance shipments to Mexico freed up millions more. Top management was looking for every possible new source of cash and was taking actions — like slowing payments to suppliers — to staunch the flow of capital.

It was touch and go at times. Nevertheless, the vigilance helped. Since Chrysler could not rely on outside financing, and the federally guaranteed loans were earmarked for new products and the facilities to make them, Chrysler had to become its own banker for a while. It is remarkable that during this time Iacocca was approving the purchase of robots and other advanced production technology for small vans and other car models that would not be introduced for years.

Chrysler had a plan for short-term survival — aggressive cash management. Beyond that, it was looking for new sources of cash. There really was only one alternative: the sale of assets. Iacocca had long resisted the temptation to sell Chrysler's profitable subsidiary that made tanks for the military, arguing that it was the company's only line of business that did not have Japanese competition. But there were buyers willing to pay cash for a business with a guaranteed profit, and Chrysler's need was for cash now, not future profits. So the tank division was sold for $350 million in early 1982. "That took our cash reserves from almost nothing to what looked like an inexhaustible amount at the time," Miller said.

The effect was more than a gain in liquidity. It assured others that the company was no longer on the brink of failure, and it encouraged the whole system that surrounds an automobile company. "Having that big block of cash there told every supplier, 'Don't you worry about getting paid,'" said Miller. "And it said to the dealers, 'Go ahead, make the plunge. Fix up your showroom; put in more service stalls. This company is going to be around.'"

The auto market was beginning to recover at this time, so the focus began to shift from Chrysler's problems to the new products it had coming to market. The company managed to squeeze out a profit of $12.5 million in the second quarter of 1982. Lee Iacocca went to Washington to make the announcement and joyfully handed out bottles of black ink, which he said were symbolic of the company's recovery (despite losses that still lay in the future). Chrysler had weathered its cash crisis.

It had done so because the intervention of Iacocca and his newly assembled team broke the cycle of pain leading to collapse and radical change in an unmanaged crisis. Management does make a difference, especially in a case like Chrysler's, where the crisis had almost run its full course and radical change seemed near. As Yogi Berra once put it, "People said it couldn't be done. But sometimes it doesn't always work out that way."

WHEELING-PITTSBURGH STEEL

Dennis Carney had spent eight years as chief executive of Wheeling-Pittsburgh Steel Corporation, doing a creditable job of rebuilding a second-rate steel company in a rapidly shrinking industry. His successor, George Ferris, credits him with doing a "great job, putting it together the way it is." Nevertheless, on September 20, 1985, Carney was abruptly dismissed by a restless board and an unhappy major shareholder.

Allen E. Paulson, who owned 34 percent of Wheeling-Pitt's stock, had feuded for several years with Carney, whose management style was domineering. Paulson had started as an aircraft mechanic and had built up Gulfstream Aerospace, a maker of top-of-the-line corporate jets. Earlier in the year he had sold Gulfstream to the Chrysler Corporation and was free to concentrate on his investment in the ailing steel company.

Carney was locked in a bitter battle with the United Steelworkers Union at this point. He was seeking sharp wage concessions to cut costs, but the union, which had gone along with earlier concessions, balked this time and launched a strike. Carney was blamed personally by the strikers for attempting to break the union and was hanged in effigy outside his own plants. Cash was hemorrhaging and reserves were low. Union leaders said they would not deal with Carney, and no resolution of the dispute appeared possible as long as he remained. When Paulson personally agreed to guarantee Carney's substantial severance payments, he agreed to leave.

Carney had led Wheeling-Pitt through terrible times in the American steel industry. For thirty years after World War II, the industry had neglected to modernize itself and reduce costs. Suddenly it discovered that it could not match imported steel in either quality or price, and Wheeling-Pitt was no exception.

Carney had jumped to Wheeling-Pitt in 1974 from U.S. Steel, where he had been a vice president for research. His goal was to become chairman, and by 1978 he was. Carney holds a Ph.D. in metallurgical engineering from the Massachusetts Institute of Technology, and his solution to the company's problems was, not surprisingly, reliance on advanced technology. Despite Wheeling-Pitt's small (3 percent) share of the steel business in this country, he invested heavily in new facilities. The company could ill afford the $806 million he spent, particularly when the market for the products was by no means certain, and debt soared. Carney's attitude was "If you don't take the gamble of investing in modern equipment, you're ensuring your death."

But markets remained soft, and losses mounted. It did not matter that the company was becoming a highly efficient producer; its mills were running at low capacity. Credit sources began to dry up, and Carney kept turning to the well-paid members of the Steelworkers Union for concessions to limit cash outflows. At first he was successful and extracted over $100 million from union members. He was also successful in winning federal loan guarantees to build a new rail mill and in persuading bankers to ease loan terms. He sought outside investors with limited success, arranging a joint venture with Nisshin Steel of Japan in early 1984. But his harsh management style had spurred defections; four second-rank executives departed, leaving him without a successor in sight. Union leaders — and rank and file members — resented his bombastic style and demands.

Carney's cash crisis began to peak in early 1985. From 1982 through 1984 he had reported losses totaling over $170 million but was still spending heavily. Interest costs were growing more burdensome and repayments were coming due; once again he turned to the banks and union for assistance. Negotiations with both broke off but were resumed as the possibility of failure loomed larger. By early April, it looked as though a solution had been found.

The union agreed to accept a pay cut from $21.40 an hour to $19.50 — that alone would have saved $100 million in cash — and the banks agreed to defer $210 million in interest and principal payments and provide an additional $40 million line of credit. But the banks demanded a lien on $300 million of current assets. Though Carney agreed, the unions refused, and the deal fell apart. On April 16, 1985, Wheeling-Pitt filed for pre-emptive protection under Chapter 11 of the bankruptcy laws.

The filing fended off the banks for a while, but labor costs continued unabated. Carney asked a federal bankrupty judge to void the existing labor contract and slash wages and benefits 30 percent, from $21.40 an hour to $15.20. Otherwise, company officials argued, it would be out of cash by the end of the year. The judge ruled for the company, but union leaders regarded the move as the start of an attack on pay scales throughout the entire industry and began a strike on July 21. It was the first major steel strike in twenty-six years, and there was no doubt who the workers thought was the cause. Picketers chanted, "Carney must go!"

In the meantime, relations between Carney and Paulson had become frosty after some board room shouting matches. Given the extent of Paulson's stockholdings, these differences made it harder for Carney to hold a consensus together. At the end of July he asked the board for a resolution declaring its support for his handling of the strike. When an informal poll before the meeting indicated something less than unanimous backing, a director persuaded Carney to withdraw the proposal.

The strike dragged on for almost two months, with minimal contact between the two sides. By early September, it was clear that the union would not deal with Carney. "The only way to settle this thing is to have somebody else do it," one director said. Carney, sixty-four years old, said he would be willing to depart if he was given his promised golden handshake. With the company in Chapter 11, all payments of this sort would have to be approved by a judge, and the union was sure to object, but Paulson agreed to back the payments personally, and Carney resigned, along with five other directors.

Like Chrysler, Wheeling-Pitt's cash crisis was of the most serious kind. The environment was largely shaped by outside forces, including foreign competition, the strong dollar, and federal regulations. And the precrisis had been building for years: a poor market coupled with extremely high outlays on new facilities had been factors for some time. So the cash crisis was in a very mature stage when Paulson made his move in September 1985. Wheeling-Pitt was, by the company's own admission, perilously close to collapse and radical change when the board finally acted. Ferris faults previous management for taking the stance it did and prolonging the strike. "It was strictly a misunderstanding," he said. "The union was anxious to talk and anxious to negotiate, but for some reason we didn't. We lost $100 million for nothing. A shame for labor, a shame for the company." As this is written, it is by no means certain the company will survive. Paulson's newly appointed CEO, George A. Ferris, a former executive of Ford's steel subsidiary, is optimistic. He settled the ninety-eight-day strike in short order, and has set about changing attitudes, declaring that "we may be financially bankrupt, but we will never again be morally bankrupt." We shall see, but Ferris has a good start. He delivered a surprise $4 million profit for the first quarter of 1986, only six months after taking over.

WICKES

Sandy Sigoloff was thrust into a cash crisis at Wickes Corporation on March 29, 1982, at the worst possible point — with collapse in sight. Like Lee Iacocca, he had little understanding of how deep Wickes's problems were, but it didn't take him long to find out. He had a crisis team trained from his days as the head of Daylin, another West Coast retailer that he had turned around; his first move was to reassemble that group.

Sigoloff had little advance warning that he would be grappling with Wickes's accumulated difficulties. Only ten days earlier, he had been contacted by Bernard Shapiro, a lawyer who had represented the creditors of Daylin in the mid 1970s but had become friendly with Sigoloff's former adversary. Now retained by Wickes, Shapiro explained to Sigoloff that the company's board, under heavy pressure from its lenders, had been promised the resignation of Emil L. McNeely, the incumbent CEO, and was looking for someone from the outside as a replacement. Sigoloff, a nuclear physicist by training, had acquired a reputation as a superb organizer and turnaround artist, though he lost the chance to manage a revived Daylin when he was surprised by an unexpected and successful takeover offer by W. R. Grace in 1979. Most of the Daylin management team had dispersed after the takeover (Sigoloff himself was the number two man with Kauffman & Broad at the time he was approached by Wickes), but had remained in touch with one another.

As soon as Sigoloff was offered the top spot at Wickes — three days before actually signing on — he started contacting his former associates. He wanted to have his "tiger teams" together and ready to grab hold of the company before he arrived at Wickes.

When Sigoloff arrived, Wickes was a $4 billion company, the nation's thirteenth largest retailer. It was a complex agglomeration of businesses, including twenty-three retail chains, five wholesalers, four manufacturing units, one insurance company, two credit businesses, and three leasing operations. And it was in serious trouble.

Many of the company's difficulties stemmed from its acquisition of Gamble-Skogmo, which owned a collection of old, small-town stores throughout the low-growth Midwest. "We had the wrong locations, the wrong merchandise, the wrong image, and the wrong format," Sigoloff later said Wickes's thirty-two hundred outlets. "Aside from that, it was a great business."

Wickes paid $200 million to acquire Gamble-Skogmo in 1980 and took on $990 million in debt just before interest rates began to skyrocket. The damage came quickly: Wickes lost over $500 million in the next two years. By early 1982 bills were going unpaid and shelves in stores grew bare as suppliers refused to ship without getting their money first. Customer traffic was dwindling.

When Wickes's directors offered the CEO spot to Sigoloff, he demanded, and received, over $1 million a year in salary, bonus, and benefits. More than that, he insisted on total control of management and the board. The eleven directors agreed, scarcely imagining that ten of them would be quickly ousted. "My conditions for taking on a turnaround are always the same," he said. "There is only one chief executive officer — me — and he holds all terminal decision-making authority, including authority over the board. You can't succeed in a turnaround if you have to worry about people who have ties and loyalties to the previous management."

Within days, sixty-five of Sigoloff's old associates had joined him in San Diego — then Wickes's headquarters — and had been organized into ten teams, each with its own assignment. The loyalty they demonstrated was outstanding; most quit secure jobs to plunge into a situation fraught with uncertainty. But Sigoloff knew how to build a following. When Daylin was acquired, he was given $3.5 million in stock as a reward for reviving the company. He distributed two thirds of it to employees, including clerks and secretaries, saying they were part of the turnaround team.

At Wickes, the most urgent need was to find cash: where was it coming from, where was it flowing out. Wickes's financial reporting system was a shambles, and it took precious days just to find the more than four thousand accounts the company used to collect receivables. Knowing that a Chapter 11 filing was a distinct possibility from the outset, Sigoloff ordered his tigers to try to build up a war chest in a friendly bank — one they didn't owe any money to — so that the company would have some funds to operate with if the bankruptcy option was chosen. (Banks with loans to a bankrupt company usually grab any deposits on hand to offset part of the loans, often pushing the company into insolvency and liquidation.)

After a few months of accumulating cash, Sigoloff did file for Chapter 11 protection. With debts of almost $2 billion, Wickes became the second largest bankruptcy filing in the nation's history, trailing only Penn Central.

Sigoloff next decided to rationalize Wickes's crazy-quilt structure. He lived up to his nickname, "Ming the merciless," by pushing executives into working sixteen-hour days, six and seven days a week. At one meeting he handed out stiletto-like letter openers, telling those attending that they could be used either on the envelopes holding their bonus checks or on themselves.

Sigoloff's tigers delved deep into operations, finding low morale, poorly stocked stores, years of neglected preventive maintenance. Aldens Catalogue Company, an operation of $300 million a year, was particularly troublesome. Despite Wickes's previous investment of $30 million to upgrade it, Aldens was losing $1 million a week. When no buyer could be found, Sigoloff decided to shut it down just before Christmas, softening the blow to the twenty-three hundred employees slightly by paying full severance benefits despite Wickes's Chapter 11 status.

The teams recommended selling poorly located stores and losing operations. Three hundred stores were closed and seven chains, all from Gamble-Skogmo, were sold or closed. The number of Wickes's employees shrank from forty thousand at the Chapter 11 filing to twenty-seven thousand the following January. At the same time, the tigers realized that the company's viable businesses had to be nurtured with new investments if they were to grow and flourish. Sigoloff argued with creditors that Wickes must "repay and regrow in parallel" if the company was to emerge from bankruptcy status as a strong competitor.

Sigoloff and his teams managed to stop the loss of cash by the end of the year, dropped the worst of the losers, and had formulated a short-term plan to demonstrate the intrinsic health of the company. Despite the costs of the bankruptcy proceedings and the reorganization, Wickes earned $9.5 million from continuing operations in 1983. Sigoloff was now alert to signs of executive burnout. By late 1982, he started ordering executives to take alternate Saturdays off and arranged for occasional three-day weekends to ease the pressure. Imitating Lee Iacocca, Sigoloff appeared in television advertisements for the company's leading store chains — with positive results.

By late 1983 the company had clearly begun turning the corner. The "bleeders," as Sigoloff called losing operations, had been sold or closed, and potentially successful operations nourished. A few months later, in early 1984, he persuaded the contentious creditors to agree on a reorganization plan that would pay them more than $400 million over what they would have got if the company was liquidated. By September, in what a federal judge described as "a miracle," Wickes emerged from Chapter 11.

It was a smaller company than it had been, with sales of $2.9 billion a year compared with nearly $4 billion before the bankruptcy filing, but it was healthy, with a profit of $12.2 million on sales of $806 million in the quarter preceding the settlement. After the judge approved the plan, Sigoloff handed out buttons at the company's headquarters. They said, simply, WE WON.

Sigoloff spread the good cheer. Clerical people were given the equivalent of one week's pay in cash or time off. His tigers split a bonus pool of $18 million. Though Sigoloff was in line for a bonus of close to $5 million, he didn't relax. As soon as the company was operating on a relatively normal basis, he started maneuvering to escape the fate that had befallen him at Daylin. Aware that the slimmed-down company could be an attractive takeover target, Sigoloff arranged a massive acquisition of his own less than six months after emerging from the bankruptcy proceedings.

In mid 1985, he bought the consumer and industrial products operations from Gulf & Western for $1 billion, boosting Wickes's annual sales to close to $6 billion. The acquisition gave the company such well-known brand names as Catalina and Cole of California apparel, Supp-Hose and Burlington hosiery and socks, and Simmons and Burlington mattresses and furniture. More important, it stretched Wickes's financial and management resources, making it much less attractive to potential corporate raiders.

Sigoloff used his tiger teams to manage the short-term cash crisis to keep the company alive until it could be reorganized. He put the company into the corporate equivalent of an intensive care unit, monitoring all the vital signs until it was stabilized. Managing a cash crisis does not cure the disease, but it keeps the patient alive while the fundamental causes of the illness can be located and treated. Sandy Sigoloff is a master at doing both.

More recently Sigoloff, with nearly a $1 billion potential war chest, raided National Gypsum Company, bidding $1.3 billion in cash to try his second megadollar acquisition. He was rebuffed by a management-led leveraged buy-out but remained acquisitive, saying he'll "leave the door open" and even add a fourth business to his lumber, home furnishings, and apparel domain "if we find something exciting." Exciting is the right term for Sigoloff. H. Lloyd Kaneu, from Smith Barney Harris Upham, said in early 1986, "This man ranks with the top two or three American executives today."

9

Industrial Relations
"Labor's Love Lost"

AFTER A HUNDRED YEARS of growth, the labor movement in America appears to be fading, declining under
the pressure of foreign competition, shifts in the make-up
of our economy, and the impact of deregulation. Today,
fewer than one in five nonagricultural workers are unionized. The industrial relations crisis may one day disappear
from the scene, but in the meantime, crises involving
labor can be as threatening to the life of a corporation as
any of the others we have discussed.

Industry and Labor

Industrial relations crises do not materialize out of thin
air. There is always a precrisis period; if it is detected before the blowup and action is taken, a serious disruption
can be prevented. But once the tempers flare, look out!
Strikes are a lot easier to start than to stop. Even after an
accommodation is reached — there are seldom real solu-

tions to these kinds of problems — the aftereffects can become an important part of the history for future negotiations.

Dealing with powerful unions like the United Auto Workers had become a way of life in America's industrial heartland. For a long time it didn't seem to matter that much of heavy industry had become noncompetitive in the years since World War II; management and labor were enjoying the fruits of increasing production volumes brought on by expanding domestic demand and the country's domination of world markets. Labor, powerfully unified after the desperate prewar organization struggles, had demanded continually a larger share of the profits, and management went along, if reluctantly, and watched profit margins shrink. Volume was the secret. Greater output would make up for thinner margins; who wanted to be the manager who took on a powerful union in a decisive strike?

As the United States has lost its status as the unchallenged leader and become just one of the players in the world economy, the extraordinary costs of production due to labor rates here have made one strong business after another vulnerable to low-cost offshore producers.

INTERNATIONAL HARVESTER

When people meet Archie McCardell, they come away with an impression of warmth. "Nice guy, a genuine person" is the reaction. McCardell climbed the corporate ladder easily in seventeen years at Ford and six more at Xerox, before becoming CEO at International Harvester (now Navistar International) in 1977. His rise was not surprising — he clearly had the brains, drive, and charisma to rise to the top. So the wonder is how such an experienced, capable person came to such a miserable end. Just as he approached the triumph of his career, remolding Harvester into a great company, he fell on his face. What happened? It was hard to tell in May of 1982, when he was fired less than five years after starting as president, but most of the facts are now known, and history has given us perspective.

Archie doesn't stand on pretense. When he visited my class at Carnegie-Mellon, he arrived in a rumpled gray herringbone suit and black loafers. Standing in the well of the amphitheater, he surveyed the class and then pulled off his tie. "One thing I've learned in business," he told the delighted students, "is that after five o'clock it's time to work with your collar open and your shoes off." Up to that point, all the students in the room thought they had him figured out: a hard-boiled, cigar-chomping, butt-kicking manager who had underestimated the determination of a union as powerful as the UAW and overestimated the support he could have expected of a jittery board.

McCardell said he faced three simultaneous crises at Harvester; they involved his company, the entire agricultural-implement industry, and his personal self-respect. By the time he had finished telling us his story, it was clear that there were no cardboard characters in the Harvester drama; that both sides had wound up fighting a war neither wanted, to their mutual detriment.

McCardell had been recruited from Xerox by Brooks McCormick, the last of the family that had founded Harvester in the nineteenth century and dominated it ever since. McCormick recognized that the company's new product development programs were lagging behind competitors', that the ranks of management were bloated, and that inefficient work practices, which had formed over the years, were sanctified by a contract with the UAW. "The company has not earned the cost of capital for years," observed Donald Lennox, McCardell's successor. "We were in a slow liquidation kind of business." The solution, McCormick thought, was to bring in someone from the outside, someone not wedded to the past practices and without any social ties or loyalties to the existing structure. Tough cost cutting was needed, and McCardell seemed the man to do it. To lure him away from a comfortable existence at Xerox, Harvester offered him a $1.5 million signing bonus and gave him a $1.8 million loan to buy Harvester stock, with the proviso that the loan could be forgiven if certain performance goals were met. Later, the CEO's financial package would be a central issue in the battle with the union and would eventually lead to McCardell's ouster.

Harvester had had an unsteady relationship with organized labor for a long time. In the early years, some of its plants were organized by the UAW, some by the Farm Equipment Workers Union. In 1952 the company tried to change work rules in the plants organized by the latter union, and its members walked out for nine weeks. The company won that confrontation, breaking the union, but instead of being conciliatory in victory, the company "bragged about it," recalled Pat Greathouse, now a retired vice president of the UAW. "They made a great to-do about how they'd forced a breaking of the strike, how they'd forced the people to go back to work with contracts that were decimated and with conditions that were forced upon the workers." But what the company's success did was give the UAW the opening it needed to organize the old Farm Equipment Workers plants. After that, Harvester had to contend with a single union, whose leaders had long memories.

There was another strike in 1958, one that again lasted

for nine weeks. According to Greathouse, it began in response to "a long laundry list of demands" that were presented by the company as measures to improve productivity but were interpreted by the suspicious workers as "give-backs." The company eventually backed down and tried to establish new relations with the union. There were, indeed, twenty years of labor peace, but the price was a ballooning cost structure. When McCardell arrived, he found an agricultural-implement industry that was uncompetitive in the world market and a company that was uncompetitive with its domestic rivals.

McCardell decided that his principal job was to cut costs, and shortly after arriving he started to hack away. Within six months, he had sliced three thousand people from Harvester's corporate staff and had tightened controls over purchasing. He was well on his way to his goal of cutting $500 million a year from company expenses. But, as he now admits, he was not spending enough time in the plants, not listening to the fears that were being talked of by the company's thirty-five thousand factory workers, who saw his program less as a corporate rejuvenation than as a threat to their standard of living. "I should have spent a lot more time in the plants talking with people earlier than I did," McCardell now says. If he had been in the plants, he would have seen workers sporting prominent SCREW ARCHIE buttons. Over the years, Harvester employees had learned to enjoy homes of their own, nice cars, the latest appliances, long vacations, cradle-to-grave health coverage, cheap insurance, and easy work. They had bargained for years to get these benefits; they liked them and intended to keep them. But everything depended on the preservation of the union contract. An attack that broke it would endanger the good world it had brought and the family life of the workers.

In fact, McCardell was planning just such an attack. He

cast the plan in terms of righting past wrongs, of eliminating costly practices that had been written in by previous managers who had sought labor peace at any price. Union leaders complained that McCardell and Warren Heyford, the tough president he had recruited, were outsiders who did not understand how to deal with unions or the background of labor relations in the agricultural-implement industry. "Neither of them knew anything about the industry and apparently didn't put out much effort to learn anything about the industry," snorted Greathouse. What was worse was that McCardell never attempted to talk to the union to lay some kind of groundwork for resolving work-rule disputes before the ritualized confrontation of formal contract bargaining began. The union signaled its determination in 1978 with a five-week strike at a plant in Louisville over a minor, piecework dispute. McCardell was unswayed; the union was next on his hit list.

He prepared for battle. He was anticipating a strike and the plants were run hard to build a sixty-day backlog of products for the dealers. McCardell thought the strike would last two months, and the inventory would shield the dealers from the impact of the walkout. McCardell had decided that work rules were the principal competitive difference between Harvester and the other American truck and ag-imp (agricultural-implement) companies, and he was determined to change them. He demanded the right to schedule mandatory overtime on Saturday — something that is standard in other parts of the industry but had been voluntary at Harvester for thirty years. And he wanted to reduce workers' freedom to shift from job to job, a cherished employee option but one that cut productivity and drove up costs. In the fall of 1979, McCardell's program seemed to be working: the company earned $427 million in the year ended October 31, up from $187 million in 1978. But the union was braced for battle. The company had put its demands on the table, saying they would be there "when the strike started and when it was over." The union saw no reason to compromise; on November 1 the workers walked out.

McCardell now says he was in the forefront of the trend that saw workers at such well-heeled giants as General Motors and Ford agreeing to wage and benefit cuts. He has said, "I think we were the first company to go to a union and ask them to give something up." All the union could see at the time was a concerted union-busting drive. With a $300 million strike fund to draw on, and a tradition of standing up to corporate bullies, the union was determined not to give in. As the test of strength went on, though, circumstances changed, undermining McCardell's assumptions. Interest rates began to shoot up, depressing sales of trucks and farm equipment, but McCardell felt under little pressure to settle. His anticipated sixty-day supply of products had become a four-month supply. "There was no point in bringing the workers back," he recalled; "we'd just have had to lay them off again." But Harvester was borrowing heavily to sustain the company during the strike, boosting its short-term indebtedness from $442 million to over $1 billion as interest rates soared. The union hit hard at McCardell's bonus and loan, focusing its attention and anger on the person it felt had provoked the costly conflict.

For several months the two sides refused even to talk. Finally, with spring approaching, McCardell acted to end the stalemate. The union gave in on a few demands, and work resumed under a new three-year contract on April 20, 1980. But McCardell could claim no victory. The company was staggering under its $2.2 billion total burden of debt, and for the first time in modern history, all three of its markets — trucks, construction machinery, and farm equipment — had dropped off sharply. Nevertheless, in August the Harvester board forgave McCardell his $1.8 million loan, further outraging union workers and souring the atmosphere for future negotiations. The rating agencies began downgrading Harvester's debt, and by March 1981 the company was in default of some short-term loans and seeking a restructuring of its debt. McCardell's payments, particularly the forgiven loan, had become what he described as a "public relations, employee relations" crisis in itself. "We lost more credibility over that than you'll ever know," McCardell told my students. Even the banks read newspapers, he said, and some refused to restructure loans to a company that seemed to be lavishing lush payments on a management with lackluster performance.

McCardell recognized that his compensation had become a focal point for arguments over loan renegotiations and union concessions and sought a way to "unwind" the arrangement — without costing him any money. The industry slowdown continued, and McCardell started selling parts of the company to raise cash. With a poor credit rating, he was cut off from the commercial paper and debt markets, but as his dependence on the banks increased, the banks began to exert more control over Harvester's management. The union seemed to want McCardell's scalp in return for agreeing to a wage freeze and benefit concessions, and in May 1982 McCardell was out as chairman. McCardell agreed to resign as the only way to keep the money he had been paid.

McCardell claimed that the assault on the union was an investment in the company's future, but his misreading of blue-collar determination — he later conceded that support for the strike increased as it lengthened, rather than weakened, as he had expected — and the steep slump of the economy had crippled the company. His successors have sold its construction and farm-equipment businesses, shrinking it back to just the manufacturing of trucks, in a desperate effort to keep the company alive. McCardell's unmanaged industrial relations crisis certainly produced radical change.

McCardell was both unlucky and out of touch with the plant floor. He took over Harvester just as farmers were headed into a depression; he was trapped in a strike that he had planned as a brief confrontation but that turned into a war of attrition when the demand for production dried up. The shrunken remains of Harvester are vulnerable to competition from imports because many of the underlying problems of the cost structure were never solved. McCardell now says that Douglas Fraser, then the president of the UAW, Pat Greathouse, and other union leaders understood the changing nature of the market, but were unable to convince the membership of the need for change. Pat Greathouse agrees to an extent. "Obviously the union was not blameless," he concedes. "There were some areas where compromises should have been worked out." McCardell's fundamental mistake was to lay down a challenge to a union membership unconvinced of the need for change; his misfortune was being in the wrong place at the wrong time. Even Iacocca was ultimately bailed out by a return of the car market. Harvester — or what is left of it — is still waiting.

PAN AMERICAN

In the early years of intercontinental aviation, Pan American World Airways was this country's "chosen instrument" of airborne transportation to the rest of the world. In what was then the tightly regulated airline business, it was the airplanes bearing the round blue Pan Am symbol that took off from cities on the East and West coasts of America to touch down many hours later in exotic foreign locations. As foreign airlines grew stronger, though, Pan Am faced greater competition, and with deregulation came hordes of low-cost American carriers eager to poach on Pan Am's best routes.

A company that had advertised itself as the "world's most experienced airline," and prided itself in delivering its passengers to out-of-the-way places with a touch of class, discovered that many travelers found cut-rate fares more attractive than silver-haired pilots and gracious meals. The company was beset with an overwhelming cost structure and a lack of domestic routes to feed its international flights. The acquisition of National Airlines in 1980 provided a few such routes, but it also brought more high-wage employees and an additional burden of pension costs that the competition — new, start-up airlines — would not have to pay for decades.

By 1981, Pan Am was near bankruptcy. Aware that the company might go under, Pan Am's unions accepted wage cuts of 10 percent, and a year later they agreed to continue a wage freeze in return for 10 percent of the company's stock. That helped to keep Pan Am going, but C. Edward Acker, the former Braniff and Air Florida chief brought in by Pan Am's board to preside over a restructuring of the company, realized in early 1985 that further cuts would be needed to break the cycle of losses that had totaled $650 million in the previous three years.

Many of Pan Am's financial problems were out of management's control. The strong dollar was hurting the company badly, because tickets were sold in devalued local currencies and overseas expenses were recorded in dollars. For a company whose international operations made up 80 percent of its business, this was no small matter. But labor agreements were under management's influence, and since wages and benefits had begun to creep up to prior levels, they were ripe for trimming.

Acker's problem was that Pan Am was healthier in early 1985 than it had been during the earlier rounds of bargaining. Simple survival was not at issue, although the long-term health of the airline certainly was. So Acker provoked an industrial relations crisis to get the unions to do something that is impossible without the threat of a crisis. All unions are ultimately political organizations, and unless the membership is convinced of the absolute need for concessions, they will be quick to dismiss union leaders who recommend them. The company played hard ball, incurring a month-long strike from the mechanics' Transport Workers Union, its first in twenty years. When it came time to deal with the flight attendants, the company began a widely publicized hiring and training campaign, saying it was prepared to replace strikers in short order. The company played on the fears of the older female flight attendants, suggesting that it really wanted them out of the way so that it could hire more attractive, younger women. "Nineteen, pretty, single, and cheap" was the way the flight attendants' union bulletin described the recruits.

It was not the most pleasant of undertakings, but it worked. The unions realized that an extended strike might kill the airline, and most of their members did not have skills that would pay them as well in other occupations. The company's tactics made the members angry, but also intensified the pressure on them to accept one of the key terms of the final settlement, a two-tier wage system, according to which newly hired flight attendants would be paid less than those already employed. The agreement meant that those voting on the contract did not have to take the unhappy step of cutting their own pay, but the company had the attractive prospect of decreasing its labor costs as turnover brought new people onto the staff. While labor bitterly resents two-tier contracts, some economists say they are a relatively palatable way of adjusting to the new competitive realities in industries, like airlines, where wages and costs have risen to intolerable levels.

CONTINENTAL

Frank Lorenzo tried a different approach to the problems posed by deregulation when he took over Continental Airlines. Lorenzo, who had built up Texas Air as a low-cost, low-fare carrier, decided that negotiations to revise union contracts would be futile. He touched off a crisis in September 1983 by filing for Chapter 11 status, repudiating all of his labor contracts and slashing wages in half. President Phillip Bakes claims that he declared bankruptcy because the company was out of cash. But there is little doubt the central reason was to void its union contracts. It was a daring gamble and one he probably would have lost if the national economy had been stronger. It was also a novel use of the bankruptcy law, putting the fate of the company in the hands of a single judge.

The unions, sensing an attack on their painfully exacted wage structure throughout the entire airline industry, promptly struck, crippling the airline. To coax people back to their jobs, Lorenzo had to count on the lack of other airline jobs and the atmosphere of crisis, which helped convince employees that the company was cutting wages because of real need, not malice. It was a bitter battle. Workers crossing picket lines were harassed and physically attacked. New pay packages were designed to make employees partners in the airline's operations; profit sharing was to give workers a direct financial interest in the welfare of the company, and pilots were offered gain-sharing payments for saving fuel by following computerized flight plans.

Gradually workers drifted back without a settlement, and Continental's operations resumed. Within two years, one third of the pilots were back at work, many of them convinced that the national union was ready to sacrifice them to uphold wage levels in the rest of the industry. Flight attendants and ticket agents came back also, and the trimmed-back Continental earned a profit of $50.4 million in the first six months of 1985, in contrast to the huge losses of the previous three years. The Machinists and Flight Attendants unions tossed in the towel in April 1985, ending their strikes and returning to work with little but their seniority intact. The strike of the rest of the pilots continued, but with lessening impact.

Though still beset by lawsuits from the unions, Continental prepared a plan of reorganization to bring it out of Chapter 11 in 1986. Lorenzo correctly sensed that deregulation had changed the power equation in the airline industry, favoring management instead of the unions. The public was eager to fly at cut-rate fares, and the only way to offer those was to bring down labor costs. Unlike Archie McCardell, Lorenzo had plenty of demand for his product as long as he could provide it. By withstanding the initial impact of the strikes and convincing at least some of his employees that the crisis was real, he saved Continental. Indeed, the publicity surrounding the labor battle at Continental helped attract public attention to the struggling airline. "We wouldn't have chosen that advertising," Bakes commented, "but it was there. The spotlight was there. Until then we were a company like Johnson & Johnson that tried to stay away from the press. We were listening too much to our lawyers."

Labor crises are always difficult, but if they are properly managed, they can provide positive results, as the induced labor crises at Pan Am and Continental appear to demonstrate.

UNITED AUTO WORKERS UNION

When I first started dealing with labor crises and the UAW, Pat Greathouse was the union's vice president in charge of matters dealing with American Motors. The union is organized in such a way that different companies come under different officers. Because General Motors and Ford are so large, each has a vice president all to itself; AMC was grouped with agricultural-implement companies. Pat Greathouse was in charge of negotiations with these companies and acted as the union's industrial relations crisis manager when the talks broke down. He was an old-time pro who came out of the bare-knuckle days of union organizing. He is retired now, but has left an indelible stamp on a beleaguered industry.

Pat's method of negotiating was to say very little and just keep pushing for more than was in the previous contract. That way he didn't give up anything and could be pretty well assured of a majority ratification vote on the new agreement from the rank and file. He was a master at manipulating weaker companies. If it looked as if a little more pressure was needed to get things moving his way, he would walk away from the negotiations, board a plane for his home in Belleville, Michigan, and stay there until he got what he wanted. I never felt that I was in a give-and-take contest with him — it was all give. The UAW never once made an economic proposal or counterproposal in my time. It was always "Your last offer is rejected. We await your next."

I'm sure that Archie McCardell had the same problem

with Pat's tactics as I did, which is probably one reason that he decided to take on the union in all-out battle. Had he been successful, it would have been a first for all concerned, but success was never likely at the weakest company in the ag-imp industry. Greathouse had shrewdly settled in advance with John Deere and the stronger companies and then hunkered down for the test of wills with McCardell.

Twice, I tried to change the UAW's insistence on excessive costs at AMC. The first time was in 1977, shortly before negotiations on a new contract were to begin. I asked Pat to meet quietly with me and Richard McCracken, my vice president for industrial relations, in the Marriott Hotel at Detroit's Metropolitan Airport to go over our thoughts on a new agreement before formal negotiations began. To my surprise, he accepted. He didn't come alone, though; he showed up with Art Shy, his administrative assistant, in tow. (A union leader will bring someone so that he can never be accused of selling out the membership in private meetings with management.) I went over my ideas on how the negotiations should go, deliberately stating the company's final financial limits in ambiguous terms.

Pat listened. I kept talking. He listened some more. Then he got up, smiled, shook my hand, and departed, uttering hardly a word. I felt that I had made a terrible mistake. He knew where I was headed, but I was still totally in the dark about his intentions. Had the old bird taken me to the cleaners? Not so, as it turned out. He understood exactly where my interests lay and knew what was and what was not possible. We had established a basis for negotiation.

AMC's negotiations with the UAW that year went well and according to script because Greathouse had my road map and knew my limits. There was the usual drama, including a walkout by the union at a critical moment, but the final result was acceptable. It was never easy for Greathouse to keep the rebellious AMC locals under control, since they seemed to enjoy raising hell with their own leaders as much as the company.

The obstacle to progress at AMC was that we had no credible way of instigating a crisis that would force movement on the union's part. The UAW correctly assumed that we were not suicidal. Yet, unlike GM or Ford, we could not threaten to move work elsewhere unless costs were trimmed; until our link-up with Renault, we had nowhere else to go.

The auto companies and others in heavy manufacturing are waging a long and difficult campaign these days to reform antiquated work rules and other union practices at the plant level. Their most effective tactic is a form of provoked crisis. Top union leaders have made it clear that it is political ruin for local leaders to advocate work-rule changes while a plant is busily producing products. But all products have life cycles, and as a product nears the end of its cycle, a company can make work forces at plants "bid" for the next product. The new one will be made on different, more modern machinery, the workers are told, and unless work rules are changed to accommodate the new system, the product will be "outsourced" — sent to a different plant or a different country. With this kind of pressure, and without the glare of publicity that accompanies national contract negotiations, unions and companies are slowly changing inefficient practices. Industrial relations crises thus can bring great harm or substantial benefits, depending on how they are managed.

10

Hostile Takeover
"Circle the Wagons"

ANYONE MANAGING a publicly traded company may have to fight off an unwanted takeover assault at almost any time. Some takeovers are genuine attempts to create value through mergers; others are simply efforts by raiders to take advantage of low stock prices to loot companies' assets. "Greenmailers" use the threat of a takeover to force worried managers to buy back their shares at inflated values. A takeover battle is sudden, jarring, and the most visible crisis that a top executive is called on to manage. Fortunately, it is also the form of crisis that has been most closely studied and best understood.

BENDIX

Bill Agee bet his company and lost. When the smoke cleared after one of the most tumultuous takeover battles of recent times, he not only had failed to acquire a company he had coveted, but had lost his own. He had also lost his job and damaged his reputation. The chain of events was complex, the speed of the action breathtaking, and the characters like those in a James Bond novel. It was the closest thing to prime time television to be found at the upper reaches of the corporate world. All the elements of a heavy-breathing drama were present: sex, megabucks, deceit, power, good guys and bad, envy, and greed. But the crux of the story was that an unfriendly attack by an unprepared aggressor was repelled by a group of well-prepared executives at the target company, Martin Marietta. They had a crisis team established well in advance and a crisis plan to follow. The message of the affair is simple enough; the action was not.

William H. Agee was a boy wonder who seemed to be blessed by good luck. No sooner had he been named president of Bendix Corporation than W. Michael Blumenthal, the chairman, was chosen as secretary of the treasury for the incoming Carter administration. That vaulted Agee into the top spot as chairman and CEO in January 1977; he was thirty-nine years old.

Agee's background was in finance, and he had little interest in the details of Bendix's operations in automotive components, aerospace, and building materials. To him, they were assets to be bought and sold as needed to ensure short-term financial performance. If he had any overriding aim, it was to direct the company away from its roots in the automotive industry and toward the more glamorous world of high technology. Developing high tech in-house would be much too tedious; Agee would achieve his goal by divestiture and acquisition.

In 1979, as Agee was developing his plans, a new player appeared on the scene. Mary Cunningham, recently graduated from the Harvard Business School, was hired as Agee's executive assistant. The two quickly became inseparable, though both maintained that their relationship was strictly business. Others in the company knew better. "It all went to hell the day that girl walked in here," said one former high-ranking Bendix executive, who suddenly found himself walled off from the CEO. "He clearly considered her to be the most brilliant strategist on his team and he told that to anyone who would listen." Within fifteen months of joining the company, Cunningham was the vice president for strategic planning. But the couple's personal involvement was trickling into the gossip columns; sniggering items about the dashing young corporate chieftain and his cute but brainy associate demoralized lower-level executives at the company, who wondered whether their operations would be sold off as a result of pillow talk. The whispers became an uproar, so loud that Cunningham was forced to resign in 1980, but she remained Agee's major influence, and they were married in June 1982.

At Bendix, Agee had piled up a war chest of $500 million in cash by selling off assets. Before going shopping, he eliminated dissent within his own ranks by forcing out four independent directors, who, he said, had potential conflicts of interest. The action rendered the board less effective as an objective appraiser of Agee's actions. He also got rid of William Panny, his president, and a vice president who might have acted as a stabilizing influence in a fast-moving crisis.

It was no secret that Agee was on the prowl for a high-technology company, and the likely objects of prey knew who they were. His first move came in early 1982, when he bought 7.3 percent of RCA and said he had only "investment intentions." Nobody believed him — certainly not RCA. He now says that he knew Bendix lacked the financial capacity to take over RCA but hoped the purchase would promote friendly talks. RCA's response was anything but friendly. The company signaled that it was prepared for all-out war. Thornton Bradshaw, RCA's chairman, issued a press release saying that Agee had "not demonstrated the ability to manage his own affairs, let alone someone else's." Both the stinging reference to Cunningham and RCA's bristling defenses worked: Agee backed off.

After licking his wounds for a few months, Agee selected a new prey — Martin Marietta. Gaining control of the major aerospace firm and defense contractor would enable him and Bendix to scale the heights of new technology. On August 25, 1982, with Agee's hostile tender offer for control of Martin Marietta, the battle was joined.

The assault on Martin had been planned largely in the chairman's mind. Agee had not built a team within the company good enough to provide him with backup assistance and to suggest alternatives if things got rough. He had hired expensive investment bankers — as is customary in a situation like this — but he did not share his thoughts with them. And he had left his own position unfortified. Bendix was at a disadvantage because it was incorporated in Delaware, which allows a majority stockholder to change the board of directors immediately. Martin was a Maryland corporation, which meant that a new majority owner had to wait at least ten days before changing the directors. Moreover, Bendix did not have staggered terms for its directors, another chink in its armor.

Agee now concedes that he misread Thomas Pownall, CEO and chairman of Martin Marietta, and the top management of Martin. "I underestimated their resolve and how far they would go" to defend the company's independence, he says. Pownall was an operations man who was deeply proud of the company's accomplishments in high technology. To him, the company, with its close ties to the military and aerospace communities, was more than a collection of assets. He considered Agee a raider who would happily break up the organization for a few more percentage points of short-term return on assets. He was also repelled by Agee's personal life and what he saw as his bad judgment.

Pownall decided to fight. He was well prepared to do so, having lined up $900 million in available credit and an investment banker primed for a defense. He had a crisis team of lawyers, bankers, and communications experts on hand to assist. They fired back at Agee: "It would be harmful for Martin Marietta's aerospace business to pass into the hands of a management lacking deep experience and continuity in the major systems business."

When it became clear that Agee wanted nothing less than control, Martin counterattacked. It rejected the Bendix offer and announced its tender of $75 a share for 50.3 percent of Bendix's stock, for a total of $1.8 billion. The business community watched in amazement as the two companies prepared to devour each other, and the phrasemakers came up with a catchy name — the Pac-Man defense. Whichever company got control first, it seemed, would survive, but with a crippling debt. Pownall also called on the assistance of an old friend, the formidable Harry Gray of United Technologies to make a parallel bid for Bendix, the two having decided in advance how to share the prize. Until then "our offer for Bendix was not particularly credible," said Frank Menaker, Martin's general counsel. "It was pretty hard to make arbitrageurs believe we were going to win this fight. When Harry Gray said he wanted to get into the act we said 'come on' because Harry was credible."

Now Bendix was on the defensive. Agee let it be known in the investment community that Bendix was for sale at the right price, a typical response of an asset manager, but one that made him appear vacillating in comparison with the steely resolve of Pownall. Bendix upped its offer for Martin Marietta shares $5, to $48 a share, but at the same time provided enormous golden parachutes for its top executives and tried to put some defensive measures into its corporate charter. Once again, the signals from Bendix indicated weakness and indecision. Agee was even compelled to hold pep rallies to try to keep Bendix employees, who controlled 23 percent of the company's stock, from tendering to the attackers.

As Agee was losing control and his crisis was mounting, he sought to meet directly with Pownall to halt what had been dubbed the "doomsday machine" — Martin Marietta's pledge to buy the Bendix shares, regardless of what happened, unless Bendix withdrew. According to press accounts, Agee was accompanied by Mary Cunningham at one of these vital face-to-face encounters. Her presence, and the obvious influence she exerted over Agee, only stiffened Pownall's resolve not to let his company fall under Bendix's control.

By late September each company had purchased a controlling interest in the other, but the issue of management control was tied up in the courts. Agee sought a way out by trying to sell both companies to Allied Corporation. But with Martin holding the majority of Bendix stock, Allied's chairman, Edward Hennessy, cut a deal with Pownall to buy the Bendix stock in his control. Bendix would be merged into Allied, but Martin Marietta would remain independent, and Allied would hold 39 percent of its stock. Martin Marietta later made arrangements to repurchase the stock, ensuring its complete independence.

As usual, little remained unchanged after the crisis. Hennessy quickly swept out Agee and Alonzo L. McDonald, his hand-picked president. Pownall was forced to sell off some of Martin's operations to reduce the debt it had run up during the battle. And because it was a fire sale, Bendix stockholders got a little more than ten times the annual earnings, not a particularly good price, though most seemed happy with $85 a share.

To this day, Agee insists that what he did was right, that it well served his executives, with a few exceptions, and resulted in ample reward for the stockholders of Bendix. That, he says, is what counts. But when he is pressed, as he was in my class at Carnegie-Mellon, he expresses regret at the terrible public relations, which has made him anathema to corporate leaders; he calls the transaction "the most misunderstood deal of our time." His claim of success rests on the assertion that "it was good for the shareholders, good for the employees, many of whom were shareholders and few of whom were fired, and the resulting company ended up bigger, stronger, and more diversified."

In spite of the headlocks Bendix and Martin had on each other near the end, Agee said he felt "in control" of the process until some of his directors resigned rather than remain entangled in the mess. He also said he felt let down by his lawyers, who did not tell him in advance of Bendix's legal disadvantage vis-à-vis Martin. He had rejected the "poison pill" (suicide) financial defense and a long-tenured staggered board by-law change on ethical grounds, but says he told his lawyers he wanted to fight Martin Marietta with "everything else. I thought it was done. But it wasn't. It was a screw-up, a big fundamental mistake."

He says the reason Tom Pownall is still running Martin Marietta while he is managing a personal company, Semper Investments on Cape Cod, is due to a double-cross by Hennessy. But the fact remains that he started the fight and ended up outgunned and outsmarted.

The Bendix crisis is somewhat unusual, since it was self-imposed, but otherwise it follows a typical path. It was slow in getting under way and then rapidly accelerated, reached a climax when the doomsday machine went into operation, and wound up with radical change, the absorption of Bendix into Allied. Agee's protests to the contrary, the Bendix side of the case has all the markings of an unmanaged crisis.

Martin Marietta, on the other had, started with a serious disadvantage, since the attacker had surprise and enormous momentum in his favor. But the superb performance of Pownall's crisis management team, gave it the victory. The lesson is clear: the most effective protection against hostile attack consists of preparation, strategy, and resources.

TRANS WORLD AIRWAYS

The players are more important than the plays in the "hostile takeover" game. It is essential to find out who is in on the action and to know the track record and behavior characteristics of the players. Indeed, once you have a fix on the people involved, it is fairly easy to predict the course of a takeover crisis and the likely outcome.

Take, for example, the takeover of TWA, once one of the nation's foremost airlines, by Carl Icahn, who had been best known as a greenmailer, buying up large chunks of a company's stock in the usually successful hope that terrified managers would buy them back at a higher price. When Icahn made his first move on TWA in the spring of 1985, there was no reason to believe that his tactics this time would be any different. But two other players were to change the outcome drastically: Frank Lorenzo, the man who broke the unions at Continental Airlines and converted it into a low-fare carrier, earning organized labor's undying enmity in the process, and C. E. Meyer, the quiet, nonconfrontational accountant who was chairman of TWA. The mixing of these dissimilar personalities was the real story of the TWA takeover crisis, overriding the machinations of the investment bankers and the rhetoric of the merger and acquisition lawyers.

Carl Icahn is an unusual man. An only child, raised in Queens, New York, he was a self-taught chess expert as a youth and managed to work his way through Princeton while studying philosophy. He went on to medical school, but dropped out after three years when he realized that his interests were elsewhere. Heading for Wall Street, he started as a stockbroker with Dreyfus in 1961 and by 1968 had founded Icahn & Company, an independent brokerage. Icahn is not an organization man; by his own admission he likes rocking boats. His attitude is that many chief executives are the products of a flawed process: "In a lot of corporations a guy gets to the top by kowtowing, and then picks someone to succeed him who has done the same thing." One of his childhood heroes was the ultimate corporate maverick and aviation pioneer Howard Hughes — a clue, perhaps, that his intentions toward TWA involved more than greenmail or liquidation. In fact, when he finally did take control of the airline, he donned the black and gold military-style jacket of Captain Harry R. Hoglander, the head of the pilots' union, and shouted, "We've got ourselves an airline! We've got ourselves an airline!" This was clearly more than just another deal for Carl Icahn; it was the fulfillment of a lifelong dream.

Frank Lorenzo was on a different track. A Harvard-educated lawyer, he had taken advantage of airline deregulation and the bankruptcy laws to engineer what some described as the "biggest expansion in airline history" when he combined his Texas Air with faltering Continental. He had increased traffic and profits and was laying plans for a new regional airline. He was on a roll, but he had made powerful enemies. The airline unions were still bitter about his use of Chapter 11 to break the labor contracts at Continental and ultimately the unions themselves. One observer has called him "an absolute genius," but Vern Countryman, a professor at the Harvard Law School, says his tactics are "the biggest abuse of Chapter 11 I've seen yet." He is described by *Business Week* as a "ruthless pragmatist whose only close friends are business associates. And they don't last long."

In contrast to the flamboyance of Icahn and Lorenzo, C. E. Meyer, Jr., kept out of the public eye and is careful about what he says and does. An MBA and a certified public accountant, he is a true financial type, who spent five years as senior vice president for finance at TWA before moving up. He had a reputation for talking tough with labor but giving in when the pressure mounted. At a time when the industry was being rocked by the changes of deregulation, he agreed to a settlement in 1983 that increased the wages of mechanics and flight attendants by 30 percent, pushing TWA's labor costs even farther out of line with the rest of the industry. He was not interested in selling TWA and initially tried to fend off Icahn, whose early bid he described as "uninvited and undesirable." But he pledged only to "take all appropriate steps" to defend the airline against a takeover, a response that was hardly in the same league as Tom Pownall's bet-the-company, scorched-earth resistance to Bendix. His management of the company was described as lackluster, where simply matching industry averages was considered adequate performance. One Texas Air executive described TWA as the kind of place where top executives "rush out at four-thirty to beat the peons out the door at five." To me, the atmosphere at TWA sounds like Chrysler be-

fore Iacocca; the company was ripe for a raid, and Carl
Icahn was at the door.

The first reports that Icahn was making a move on TWA
began to be heard in late April 1985. He was moving fast,
not taking the usual route of buying 5 percent and then
discussing a tender. In May he disclosed that he already
owned 20.5 percent of the stock and was looking for more.
Meyer's reaction was to hire an investment banker to find
a white knight and to argue with government authorities
that Icahn's past as a raider and greenmailer made him
unfit to run an operating business. Discussions were held
with Frank Borman of Eastern Airlines, but that company
was just recovering from its own brush with disaster and
was in no position to take on TWA's problems. The contacts made with Lorenzo exacerbated already tense relations with labor.

Meyer's search for a white knight took a bizarre turn
when he announced a deal with Resorts International, the
casino and hotel company, but four days after the announcement, Resorts admitted that it did not have the
necessary cash. Meyer started talking about a leveraged
buyout by management, since friendly suitors all were
scared off by the high labor costs, and handed out golden
parachutes to thirty top executives. By early June, Icahn
had over 30 percent of the stock, and Meyer seemed resigned to the inevitable. But then, on June 14, Meyer announced an arrangement with Lorenzo whereby Texas
Air would take over the much larger TWA for close to $1
billion. Lorenzo was also given options to buy 6.4 million
additional shares. The rationale for the deal was that
Texas Air's strong domestic operations would feed passengers into TWA's international flights.

But the unions were convinced that Lorenzo would try
the same approach as he used at Continental, converting

TWA into a low-fare carrier by cutting workers' wages and benefits. With an arbitration proceeding coming to an end, they had the strike weapon in hand and made it plain they would use it if Lorenzo took over. The unions went to Icahn and offered concessions if he would up the bidding enough to win. As one union leader put it, "Hell will freeze over before labor does business with Lorenzo. The last option is Carl. It's the lesser of two evils." Icahn pushed his offer to $24 a share, $1.00 more than Lorenzo, and kept piling up the stock, topping 40 percent in early August. Time was now a vital factor; Meyer had run out of maneuvering room. He was locked into an agreement with Lorenzo, so he couldn't look for another partner, and nothing came of meetings between the three parties to work out an amicable settlement.

As Icahn's stockholdings continued to swell, Lorenzo saw his deal slipping away. He tried to persuade Meyer to try a "crown jewel" defense by selling some of TWA's most valuable assets to Texas Air and diluting Icahn's holdings by issuing new shares. Lorenzo also snapped at union leaders' charges that a triumph by him would instantly plunge the airline into chaos.

In the end, the deals that Icahn had made with the key unions, calling for massive wage and benefit cuts in return for profit sharing and 20 percent equity in the company, won the day for him. At a decisive meeting of the TWA board on August 20, at which Captain Hoglander appeared in full dress uniform and delivered an impassioned polemic against Lorenzo, the directors turned down Lorenzo and gave the nod to Icahn.

Investment bankers said it was the first time a major stockholder in a company banded together with its unions to defeat a merger favored by management. Icahn knew his opponent; the chess player had used Lorenzo's past to outmaneuver him for the big prize. Meyer had been reduced to little more than an observer of the battle. Icahn promised to operate the airline, not to sell off its assets, as some had feared. But there is little doubt that major changes are to come. As one TWA executive put it to *Business Week,* "Whatever happens, this whole thing is a necessary rite of exorcism for TWA management. The needed changes would have never happened on their own."

Lately the attractiveness of owning TWA has faded. Not only have competitive pressures on pricing depressed earnings, but labor costs remain high and foreign travel is curtailed owing to terrorist threats. TWA is especially exposed because in 1986 it was the victim of vicious terrorism, resulting in death and injury to passengers and crews. Losses are mounting to hundreds of millions, and analysts once again are forecasting an imminent sale to another company.

CBS

From the beginning of the attack, most people knew how it would turn out. Ted Turner, "the mouth of the South," was trying to take over prestigious CBS with a package of high-risk, high-yield "junk bonds" and a well-earned reputation for flamboyance. His opponent, Thomas Wyman, the chief executive of CBS, had a proven track record of managing people and a great sense of balance. If each man lived up to his advance billing, regardless of the actions yet to take place, the victory would go to Wyman. That, of course, is exactly what happened, making the case an outstanding example of crisis management against a hostile takeover.

Tom Wyman is not a typical businessman. He majored in English at Amherst; his thesis was on the early poetry of William Butler Yeats. But he has done well in the commercial world, finding out how to operate effectively in the shadow of powerful men with distinctive personalities, such as Edwin Land of Polaroid, William Spoor of Pillsbury, and William Paley of CBS. Over the years he has learned to fight quietly and effectively — and to win. The training served him well when he slugged it out with General William Westmoreland and Senator Jesse Helms over news coverage before coping with Turner.

Wyman was ready when Turner came knocking. He had plenty of financing in place and teams of inside and outside crisis managers ready to go. The inside team included George Vradenburg III, vice president and general counsel, William Lilley III, a senior vice president, and Fred J. Meyer, senior vice president for finance. On the outside there were the noted merger and acquisitions lawyers Joseph Flom, Joseph Fogg, and Alan C. Stephenson. These were not softball players. When Senator Helms and the investor Ivan Boesky made threatening moves earlier, the lawyers went to former employees of the two to dig up potentially embarrassing information

Communications is another area of the economy where changes in the regulatory climate are altering the rules of the game. Broadcast licenses have become easier to transfer, and media companies, once protected by the Federal Communications Commission, have become vulnerable to hostile takeovers. Senator Helms put the spotlight on CBS when he formed a group of conservative investors to buy CBS stock with the avowed purpose of taking control and changing what he considered the network's biased coverage of the news. He wasn't given much chance of success, but the effort alone emphasized that CBS was just another company, that 70 percent of it was owned by institutions with no loyalty greater than a higher stock price, and that it was as open to a raid as any firm.

When Capital Cities acquired the rival network ABC in early March 1985, Wyman knew he was on somebody's hit list. Quickly, he developed a crisis plan to ward off an attacker. He arranged a $1.5 billion line of credit with Chemical Bank and drew his wagons into a circle.

The first adversary turned out to be Ivan Boesky, a noted arbitrageur. He announced that he had become CBS's largest single stockholder, with 8.7 percent of the shares. Boesky's average acquisition price was $95.50, and he offered to resell the shares to the company for $105 apiece. Wyman refused to be greenmailed and sent his lawyers into court, charging Boesky with violating securities laws while he was accumulating his shares. The legal challenge stopped Boesky, because to defend against the charges, he would have had to open his closely guarded operations to hordes of hostile lawyers.

While that action halted Boesky, other maneuvers were afoot. The danger was that Wall Street would decide that CBS was "in play" and that it was just a matter of time until a serious takeover attempt was made. Wyman sent his lawyers to the big investment banking companies, warning of conflict of interest suits if they got involved with a raider like Turner. He also took more defensive steps; for example, he had the board change a rule that permitted 10 percent of the stockholders to call a shareholders' meeting to one that allowed only the chairman, the executive committee, or the whole board of directors to call such a meeting.

When the assault from Turner did come, it was hardly a surprise; he had been talking for years about wanting to operate a broadcast network after successfully building his Cable News Network. His offer in mid April 1985 was for $175 a share, seemingly attractive for a stock that was selling for about $115. But the offer was greeted with skepticism in the all-important financial community, because there was virtually no cash involved, just a fistful of securities. Turner said his plan was to finance the purchase by selling off all activities of CBS that were not connected with broadcasting.

Wyman's team went into action. Each morning the inside group, known as the "war council," met to discuss the situation and devise tactics. "Tom was tough and kept us going," Mr. Lilley said. "He wanted every detail." The strategy was to fight the battle in the courts and regulatory agencies to delay Turner and anyone like him while the costs of the takeover effort mounted. Before the FCC, CBS questioned Turner's fitness to run a national news network; accountants hired by CBS queried the earnings statement of Turner's companies; and Morgan Stanley, Wyman's investment banker, characterized the offer as financially imprudent. At the Securities and Exchange Commission, the company outlined some of the actions it might take to resist a takeover, including diluting existing shares by issuing new stock, buying or selling assets, repurchasing stock, recapitalizing, or other business strategies.

Boesky was the first to sue for peace; he sold half of his stake and pledged not to participate in a takeover or proxy fight at CBS for a period of years. CBS, in return, dropped its lawsuit against him.

The network's political clout was used to pressure the FCC to delay approval of Turner's fitness to operate CBS's broadcast properties. Meanwhile, in the state capital of Albany, the advance of a bill to block hostile takeovers was another obstacle in Turner's path. Then Wyman delivered the knockout punch. He proposed buying back 21 percent of the company's stock for $40 in cash and $110 in notes and putting limits on the amount of debt the company could incur. The move thwarted Turner, although he didn't give up immediately, and took CBS out of play for a while. Marvin Davis, the billionaire oil magnate, attacked in early 1986, offering $160 per share in cash, but was repulsed.

Turner was gambling that Wall Street's appetite for action and the popularity of junk bonds would let him take over a company he had nowhere near the means to acquire in any conventional way. Tom Wyman didn't gamble. He was prepared for a crisis, even if he didn't know exactly when or from what quarter it would come, and he had the mechanisms in place to deal with it. That's why he won.

GULF, MESA, AND CHEVRON

Now comes a tale of what *not* to do.

James E. Lee moved into the chairman's office at Gulf Corporation's Pittsburgh headquarters, in 1982, determined to increase reserves and improve operating efficiency, a standard agenda for the chief executive of an oil company. He was regarded in the oil industry as a genial man, perhaps the best liked in the business. But those aspects of his personality which made him easy to get along with seem to have prevented him from making effective decisions and taking swift action in a time of crisis.

A hostile takeover attempt, even for a $29 billion corporation that was one of big oil's Seven Sisters, should not have been unexpected. The mid 1980s were a time of acquisition and consolidation for the refining companies, with U.S. Steel taking over Marathon, T. Boone Pickens, Jr., of Mesa launching a raid on Cities Service and driving it into the arms of Occidental, Du Pont acquiring Conoco. The prevailing wisdom in the industry was that it was cheaper to acquire oil reserves through the stock market than to go through the tedious, expensive business of punching holes in the ground.

Despite this, Lee had launched high-risk exploration operations in the Arctic in hopes of hitting a big new field, sold off losing European operations to interests in Kuwait, and slashed personnel by 25 percent. The actions made the company more attractive to anyone who knew the industry but did little to improve Gulf's standing on Wall Street, where its shares continued to be held in low regard. Lee apparently thought the company was simply too big to be taken over by someone who wanted to avoid an antitrust problem.

Pickens, on the other hand, says he saw Gulf as an especially valuable prize with its huge annual cash flow of $3 billion and debt of only $2 billion. He said the company "had a very strong balance sheet and a poor management record."

The danger signals started going off in the summer of 1983, when Gulf shares began to be heavily traded. T. Boone Pickens and his partners, who had profited handsomely from raiding other companies and sending them running for white knights, was on the march; by October he had acquired 8.75 percent of the company. The reaction of Lee and the rest of Gulf's top management was incredulity mixed with anger. (Pickens told us at Carnegie-Mellon that Gulf "was a classic example of management's thinking they own the company.") In Gulf's view, Mesa, with annual sales of a little over $400 million, was simply not in the same league.

At the same time, Lee, a soft-spoken elder in the Presbyterian church, resolved not to use gutter tactics to repel the assault. "Jim was determined not to lose his principles in the process," an associate said. He flatly refused to buy back Pickens's stock or work in any way with the raider from Texas. Instead, he opted for a form of "skunk repellent" by attempting to convert Gulf from a Pennsylvania corporation to one chartered in Delaware, an action that would make it more difficult for Pickens to claim a seat on the board. Pickens engaged in a proxy fight that Gulf's management barely won, but with that victory in hand, Lee relaxed. He did nothing to change the company's capitalization to make takeover more difficult, nor did he launch a counterattack on Mesa, which most observers in the investment community felt would have succeeded. Instead, Lee said Gulf would stick to its plan to improve operations.

The delay gave Pickens, who was under intense financial pressure ("I had my back to the wall at that point"), a chance to regroup, and Lee's lack of a vigorous defense against Mesa was giving other people in the oil patch ideas as well. Robert Anderson of Arco saw a chance to get his hands on Gulf's reserves at a bargain basement price, and to Lee he proposed an acquisition at $70 a share. Lee refused, but Pickens was aware of the offer and quickly mortgaged his own properties to the hilt and launched a partial tender offer for the company at $65 a share. The turnabout stunned Lee; Gulf was in play, with money managers ready to sell for the highest bid. Lee's cool relations with the financial community did not help his cause at a crucial time.

The only entities willing to pay the price Pickens was proposing were other oil companies that were desperate for reserves. The bidding was soon reduced to Arco, Standard Oil of California (best known for its Chevron brand), and a group of managers who attempted — far too late to have much chance of success — a leveraged buyout. In the end the temptation of Chevron's $80 a share in cash was simply irresistible. At the decisive, final board meeting, Lee was described as a "broken" man who had offered little encouragement to his own team in their buyout effort. Twice, he was unprepared for an attack from the outside, failed to manage his crisis, and in the end was consumed by it.

AMERICAN MOTORS

I had my own brush with an hostile takeover at AMC. A year after I became boss, my turnaround plan was working so well that we had plenty of cash and earnings at record levels. That started to attract attention in the investment community; the price of our common stock doubled and then tripled, going from $3.00 a share to $12. On some days AMC stock was the most active on the New York Stock Exchange.

One day John Tierney, AMC's treasurer, notified me that large blocks of our stock were being bought by investors using "street names" to conceal their identity. Shortly afterward, Andrew Sage, a member of our board and managing director of Lehman Brothers, burst into my office, beaming from ear to ear. "We're being attacked," he said. "Isn't it wonderful?" AMC was like the homely high school girl who suddenly blossoms and finds herself being chased by the football heroes.

I was considerably less delighted than Andy, because we were only halfway through the two-phase strategy that had got me the top job at AMC. The first, which was well under way, was to turn the company around in financial terms; the second was to find a partner. I wanted a wealthy, international, technically sophisticated company that was willing to pay for what we had in the rich American market. If some unrelated conglomerate or takeover artist were to get hold of us before we could complete the second stage of the plan, he would get us cheap, and long-term shareholder values would suffer.

The interested buyer was thought to be Volkswagen. We had spurned its earlier offer because it was not willing to pay for our dealer network; it had its own in this country. Unsuccessful with that approach, was it trying another tactic?

The knowledge that we were under attack intensified developments on other fronts. We were talking seriously with Peugeot, which had never successfully managed to penetrate the United States market and saw our distribution network as a way of quickly broadening its presence here. The sticking point was that it was not interested in our manufacturing operations, a major part of the company. Still, we might have made a deal if I hadn't got a call as we were drawing up the agreement papers with Peugeot.

It was from François Dubins, an official of Renault, who had got wind of our prospective deal. "Are we too late?" he asked when we met a few days later. "No, but you're close," I responded. "Here's what I want." I shoved a package of papers across a conference table toward him. He riffled through the sheets, looked up, and said, "I think we can do business." Then he disappeared.

One morning shortly after, I went to New York not knowing who our new partner would be that night. A small army of lawyers, investment bankers, public relations people, and top AMC executives crowded into a suite of rooms at the Plaza Hotel. We had open telephone lines to the Pierre Hotel, where the Peugeot team was assembled, and to the Carlyle, where the Renault group had taken up residence. In the end, Renault came to terms just minutes before we were prepared to sign with its French competitor.

Anyone looking back on these events can see why I was disturbed at the prospect of having an unknown, perhaps unfriendly, attacker at the door. In fact, one of the beneficial results of our arrangement with Renault was that it did away forever with the possibility of an outside attack. Nobody would try to outbid the French government to take over AMC.

Before we had the security of the Renault deal completed, though, we did something we should have done earlier. We had a hostile takeover response plan prepared by experts in mergers and acquisitions. We went over the possible scenarios, decided what action to take in each case, lined up a crisis response team, informed the members of their duties, and so forth. We put all the information into a book, complete with the names and telephone numbers of the people who would be needed to be reached on weekends, lined up expert help, and educated our top people about the defense plans. I well remember the words I was to use if I got a call from an attacker. I was coached to say without hesitation, "Get your boxing gloves on. You're in for a hell of a fight." I was told that even if I liked what I heard, in the interests of stockholders I was to bargain for more.

So finely developed is the practice of takeover offer and response, repulse and wooing, that it has become an art form, one of the few areas of crisis management that is well developed. If all others were studied as thoroughly, we would have a fully developed body of knowledge in crisis management today. Unfortunately, takeover defense stands as a model of how far expertise in other areas has to go.

11

Adverse International Events
"Foreseeable but Uncontrollable"

THE SUMMONS to attend a meeting at General Motors'
headquarters in Detroit was as unusual as the reason for
its being called. It was April 1973 — six months before
OPEC shut the oil taps to the West — and the subject was
"energy." That evening the long rectangular table on the
fifteenth floor of the GM building on West Grand Boule-
vard was ringed by senior technical people from the auto
companies who rarely had much to do with each other. In
fact, most of us from elsewhere in the car business were
not even aware there was a fifteenth-floor conference
room. GM is run from the fourteenth floor of the massive,
gray monument planned by W. C. Durant, the founder of
the giant corporation.

GM's Science Advisory Committee was alarmed. They
had told the board chairman, Richard C. Gerstenberg,
that the company — the entire industry, for that matter — faced an "energy problem." Most of us had no idea
of what an energy problem might entail. Energy was an

intangible, an expression in physics equations. How could anyone have a problem with it? It wasn't long before I realized that the problem was a potential shortage of gasoline. This country's dependence on foreign oil had grown so rapidly that the automobile companies, most of them turning out large cars, suddenly had become subject to decisions made in the Middle East.

The thirty or so of us who listened to the presentation had mixed reactions, ranging from outright fear to heavy skepticism. I was among the skeptics. I had been hearing the oil guys cry wolf every year for the past twenty years. Their record was perfect; they were always wrong. Listening to the warning that day, I decided it was more of the same. The exporting countries needed to sell oil to feed their people. What would ever make them stop?

On October 19, 1973, I became a believer. War broke out in the Middle East, and the OPEC nations embargoed oil shipments to the Western nations. The cutoff lasted until the following March. The impact was stunning: the bottom simply dropped out of the car market. Large-car sales just died, plummeting 50 percent. GM was hit the hardest — its share of the market slid from 44.4 percent to 37.5 percent — and it closed fifteen assembly plants, laying off 160,000 workers. GM had been the dominant force in big cars, and for generations the bulk of its profits had come from the massive V-8-powered Oldsmobiles, Buicks, and Cadillacs that Americans, in the era of cheap fuel, had grown to love. Now the company was stuck with the wrong kind of product. Gerstenberg himself admitted that people were wondering whether the company would survive.

Critics of the auto industry had a field day. "Those stupid, greedy Detroit car makers had been finally caught," they crowed. The big, chrome-laden cars that Americans had driven so happily for so many years had become socially irresponsible. What most of the critics did not know, or chose to ignore, was that the biggest company in the auto industry had anticipated this international crisis and was preparing for it. GM's sin was that it had not moved fast enough.

A task force led by GM's treasurer, David Collier, had reported early in 1973 on the potential danger of the energy problem. It was this report that had prompted the meeting I attended. It had also triggered the first "downsizing" program in the company's history, started long before the cutoff. The program would lead to the shrinking of the corporation's entire product line, despite the renewed availability of fuel later in the decade. The original objective — removing four hundred pounds from the average car — was changed to drop a thousand pounds as the company assessed the gravity and probable duration of the danger. F. James McDonald, currently president of GM, says, "If we hadn't made those expenditures we wouldn't be around in 1985 and 1986," a startling confession from a man known for his candor and self-confidence. Since it takes three to five years to bring a new line of cars to market, the whole industry seemed slow to respond to the oil shortage and the enormous increase in gasoline prices.

The Japanese, who had long been making small, fuel-efficient cars for their crowded, resource-poor islands, looked like geniuses. But GM was scrambling. The onset of the fuel crisis forced it to abandon its orderly, committee approach to decision making in favor of "gut hunches" by a few people. "So much of this discussion was really instinct," said one top GM official. "The decision making was highly unstructured."

It would be hard to find a better example of how an adverse international event can set off a business crisis.

The oil cutoff took the largest manufacturing corporation in the world and stood it on its head. The entire American auto industry lost its bearings and floundered. The imports, until then mostly a nuisance, grabbed a major share of the market, apparently for good. Now, more than a decade later, the aftershocks are still being felt as the industry continues to downsize its products. And oil has become a glut on the market.

It is hard to describe how it felt to be in the middle of this chaos. As senior vice president of product and engineering at AMC, a company with limited resources, I had the daunting task of adapting AMC to the changed environment. Time was short and our options limited. These negative factors, hitting simultaneously, were the ingredients of a first-class crisis. We did have one thing going for us at AMC, though: our cars were perceived as being fuel efficient and would sell well for a while. But that would last only until the Big Three or the Japanese caught up to us with really modern hardware.

Going International

The Yom Kippur War and the OPEC oil embargo taught us in the auto industry that we really had become part of a world economy and that we were dependent on international relationships. Our nation was moving from the dominant commercial position it had enjoyed after World War II to one of interdependence with other nations. In fact, it became clear that my company could not expect to exist much longer as a relatively small assembler of motor vehicles with a modest engineering staff and limited access to cash. It would be four years before I could do anything about this frailty by finding an international partner in

Renault, but such partnerships were clearly the future course for the entire industry.

The internationalization of the American car market meant that even the Big Three were going to need a network of overseas supply sources that could produce components at much lower cost than in unionized American factories. Cooperative engineering and marketing also became necessities. I gave speech after speech around the country, saying that the number of independent auto companies was going to shrink over the next ten years because of the need for deep pockets, high technology, and access to world markets. Harold Shapiro, the young economist who had recently been installed as president of the University of Michigan, told me I was the first auto executive he had heard express this attitude. He thought I was some kind of nut on the subject. Today, though, international blending of the industry is well under way. Who could have imagined GM and Toyota in a joint car-production venture ten years ago? Independent auto companies have become all but extinct in less than a decade. About two thirds of manufactured goods in the United States are exposed to competition from abroad. When adversity strikes far away, it can have a serious impact at home, and this effect is likely to be felt even more in the future.

The new reality puts an emphasis on early detection of shifts in international tides. GM came to the realization very late, even though it was the first in the industry to do so. Being alert to what is going on outside your national borders is vital, even if you have little control over the events themselves. Having a good idea of what is going on gives you the opportunity to adjust your thinking before the waves reach the shore.

Crises born of adverse international events are among the least controllable a manager must face. They require foresight, insight, patience, and resources. Unfortunately, these qualities are always in short supply.

A KREMLIN CAPER

During the mid 1970s I was so convinced of AMC's need for international partners, product sources, and markets that I became interested even in Russia. I knew there was no point in joining forces with a Russian auto company, but there was a product or two being made there that I thought might tie in well with our Jeep line. I particularly wanted to look at a four-wheel-drive, off-road unit, which the Russians had developed by using a converted Fiat drive train and a surprisingly sleek but utilitarian body. I had the thought after talking with Armand Hammer in the late 1960s about the possibilities for American business in the Soviet Union.

To get started, I called Uri Arkus-Duntov, the businessman brother of Zora Arkus-Duntov, who was chief engineer of the Corvette sports car, and asked about doing business in the Soviet Union. He was helpful, and within a few weeks I was in an airplane headed for Moscow to meet with officials of the Soviet auto industry. They were keen on the idea of an export business in motor vehicles that would generate hard currency for their trade with the Western world. But it was my first trip to Russia — and I had a lot to learn.

It didn't bother me all that much to be met, on landing, by sullen, machine gun–toting troops in orange and olive uniforms and stiff-brimmed hats ringed with scarlet ribbon. I had got used to that kind of reception in Argentina in the days when President Arturo Frondizi was riding high after the fall of Juan Perón. What I didn't like, though, was the prison where I was sent to stay, the Intourist Hotel located not far from Red Square. From the outside it looked like Attica prison, minus the outer walls. The inside was only slightly better: tiny rooms, no amenities, and no outside contact — not even a radio. This was culture shock at its worst. At nightfall, the ancient telephone rang. It was Uri. He and his friend Vladimir would meet me for dinner at his hotel overlooking Red Square. It was wonderful to hear a friendly voice.

The three of us ate in a setting of elegant crystal and fine linen with a breathtaking view of the illuminated Red Square. We downed copious amounts of beluga black caviar, pumpernickel bread, and enough nearly frozen Russian vodka to deprive us of our senses. These fellows knew Moscow, I decided, and I figured that my life would improve if I stuck close to them. It was nearly midnight, just before the changing of the guard in front of the bright crimson towers of the Kremlin; we were ready to leave the restaurant. As Vladimir covered the check — he was a Muscovite and street smart — two very attractive women in stylish Western clothes passed our table. Uri made a pass at them, Vladimir turned purple, and I wanted to die.

Uri was smooth, I'll have to admit. After just a few minutes of conversation in Russian, he had them sitting at our table and was ordering another round of drinks. Uri was delighted. I was less than amused. Vladimir was drunk — but not too drunk to smell a rat.

We all left together just before midnight to witness the guard change at Lenin's tomb. Arm in arm, we strolled across the cobblestone square to the brightly lit center of Soviet culture. The women were plying us with questions. Names? Business? Home town? Family? Time in Moscow? Next stop? Tomorrow's appointment? At first it seemed like small talk. Then it seemed like more. "Hell," I thought, "I'm suspicious." After the spectacular thump-thump-thump of the guard change, most of the crowd quickly dispersed into the frigid night. The probing by the women continued. By now I was really concerned; these obviously were not casual pickups or prostitutes. I looked at Uri — he was giving his hotel key to the blonde. Vladimir moved in close to me. "KGB," he whispered. "Do exactly what I tell you." He hailed a cab and put Uri and the two women into it, slammed the door, and told the driver to take them to his hotel. Then the two of us ducked into the subway and sprinted for the next entrance. Vladimir didn't have to explain anything. I learned later that Uri did go to his hotel with the two women and Vladimir went to see them as well, but it was I who had been the target. If I ever see Vladimir again, I'm going to give him a medal with three oak leaf clusters. What that incident taught me was that you should know how other countries operate before trying to deal with them.

The next day was anticlimactic. I started with another blunder: at dawn I decided to jog along the Moscow River. As I trotted along, I was followed by a large Zim car — the KGB agents were not very subtle. By eight o'clock I was inside the Kremlin to meet with the high commissar of industry, machinery, and automobiles. He was a stereotype of the humorless Soviet bureaucrat, broad-faced and balding, dressed in a rumpled, Western-style wool suit, his tie askew, and his shoes unpolished. But he was the boss; Uri had done his job in setting up the meeting. I launched into my prepared speech to the big man and the group of lesser officials he had gathered in the room. I explained how they could benefit by supplying their vehicle to Jeep in North America and how we could market it and increase their volume. They, in turn, described the engineering that had gone into their vehicle, and I complimented them on the impressive unit they had cobbled together.

So far, so good. We even agreed that the biggest problem of all was the Cold War and the attitude of Americans toward the Soviet Union. If that attitude carried over to Soviet products, we would not have much of a chance, and this worried them. I agreed to research the point when I got home, but I also pointed out that the Japanese and Germans had been our enemies in World War II and that Americans were snapping up their cars and other products as fast as they hit our shores. I assured them that we could take comfort from one of America's weaknesses — a short political memory. The Russians were still doubtful when we got to the issue of price, and then I learned about the Soviets' economic mind-set and their distrust of American economic motives.

I explained how our dealers would have to get a percentage of the selling price as a "gross profit," a concept that did not have much meaning for them. In addition, Jeep Corporation would have to have 15 percent for distributing the vehicles in the United States. After freight and taxes, they would be paid in the dollars remaining. This explanation caused nothing but trouble. The Russians suspected that I was cheating them with all these "profit" figures, which have no place in their system, and the talks stalled. I decided, though, that patience would ultimately pay off, so I agreed to go home and do the market study they wanted and also do some homework to verify my profit calculations.

Some months later, Uri Arkus-Duntov called from London. He apologized for the incident of the KGB women, claiming that he had been a little drunk and had "lost his bearings." His news was that my deal was dead. Relations between the United States and the Soviet Union had deteriorated to the point that any such close cooperation in business was thought impractical. Uri died a few years later, and I never did get all the details. A CIA agent called me twice to ask what had happened, but he didn't ask the right questions.

*   *   *

The collapse of the talks with the Russians deprived Jeep of a product that could have added some badly needed broadening to its line. My own international events crisis carries its lessons. If I had kept my eyes open and my antennae out for the implications of world events, I might have had some warning of the difficulties in my path, and I certainly would have been better prepared. American business people were so isolated from the rest of the world for so long — even from events just north and south of our borders — that as a group we have not been very good at dealing with markets abroad. Like so many other things in business today, this is changing for the better, perhaps in time to save many other enterprises.

CATERPILLAR

In 1982 the best-selling business book, *In Search of Excellence,* held up a few of America's major corporations as examples of excellent performance. The message was that there were oceans of insight to be acquired by studying the way these companies approached their investments, their products, and their management practices. Caterpillar Tractor was right up there on top. Little more than two years later the company was hanging on the ropes and battling its own crisis. What happened?

Cat had been rocked by a confluence of adverse international events that overpowered the virtues lauded in *Excellence.* Sales slumped, profits turned into losses, and borrowing soared. The company was forced to abandon its premium pricing policy and go to deep discounting to try to hold on to its market share. Starting in 1982, the firm that was called the "Aristocrat of America's Heartland" by *Business Week* went from a forty-eight-year performance of continuous profits to three years of losses totaling almost $1 billion.

Caterpillar's situation has some frightening similarities with its one-time rival, International Harvester: both were plagued with overcapacity, high labor costs, and ferocious competition from overseas. Harvester, as we have seen, did not survive its struggle in any way resembling its original condition. Caterpillar stands on a stronger base, but its future is also in question.

From its earliest days, in the 1920s, when Benjamin Holt's Holt Manufacturing Company was combined with the C. L. Best Tractor Company of San Leandro, California, to form Caterpillar, the company had been known as a fanatic about quality and reliability. Most of the company's equipment is sold to contractors who lose money when their machinery breaks down. To meet their needs, the company set up a sprawling network of dealers and parts suppliers. Cat's promise was to deliver needed parts almost anywhere within twenty-four hours, and if it took as long as forty-eight hours, the part was free. This commitment to quality and good service earned the company its reputation with contractors and builders, who complete projects on time or take a financial beating. In 1925 the company's headquarters was shifted to Peoria, Illinois, and it became the largest construction machinery business in the world, with sales of $9.2 billion in 1981. Cat has been described as a national treasure for its success as an exporter: before the collapse, 35 percent of all the earth movers and related equipment in the world were painted Cat yellow.

But changes in the international environment stopped the huge machine. A deep recession and concurrent depression gripped the Third World nations that were the company's best customers, accounting for 60 percent of its sales. Many were also saddled with enormous international debts that prevented them from buying the equipment needed to build their infrastructures. Even the weakening of the world price of oil worked against Cat, since the oil exporters had less to spend on building up their industry.

At about the same time, the value of the dollar began to rise at an unprecedented rate. This pushed the price of Cat equipment, most of which is made in the United States, higher and higher, forcing overseas customers to consider other suppliers, particularly Japan's aggressive Komatsu, Ltd. For years officials of Komatsu had envied Cat's position and reputation in world markets and had copied many of its products and ways of doing business. Now it had an unforeseen advantage, a weak yen. Komatsu had been nibbling around the fringes of Caterpillar's market for years. With the dollar soaring, it plunged into the American market, Cat's stronghold, grabbing 15 percent of the $6 billion market for bulldozers and loaders by early 1985. Other foreign producers, such as Sweden's Volvo-Clark and Italy's Fiat-Alis, took advantage of the rising dollar to capture sales that in the past would have belonged to the American company. Cat management's slowness in meeting the new challenge suggests that it didn't understand the forces at work.

Even Cat's bitter battle with its workers can be traced to these international pressures. Cat's attempt to hold down its labor costs triggered a strike, on October 1, 1982, by its 20,400 union workers that lasted for 204 days, the longest such walkout in modern history. Despite its determination to put a lid on costs, the staying power of the United Auto Workers forced Cat to make a settlement far more expensive than it had intended. Not only was it unable to extract concessions like those won by Chrysler; it was forced to continue unlimited cost-of-living boosts and substitute some lump-sum payments and a profit-sharing plan for the union's traditional pay increase of 3 percent a year. The strike left the company with the worst of both worlds, a work force that was bitter about having to strike

for seven months to protect gains it had won in past contracts, and labor costs roughly twice those of Komatsu's.

Caterpillar lost $180 million in 1982, $345 million the
following year, and $428 million in 1984. Reacting to the
losses, the company started laying off employees, trimming its work force from a peak of about ninety thousand
in 1979 to about sixty thousand in early 1985. And it
began doing some things differently — abandoning some
of the practices that had earned it a place in *Excellence*.

It descended from the lofty heights of premium pricing
and started offering discounts to keep old customers and
lure new ones. Instead of producing in the heartland of
America to sell to the world, Cat sought out foreign partners and shifted production overseas when the numbers
said to do so. A new D6 tractor is being made in Grenoble,
France, rather than Davenport, Iowa, as originally
planned. Some American plants have closed completely;
others have reduced operations.

In early 1985, George A. Schaefer was installed as the
new chairman with a clear mandate to take control of the
crisis and lead the company back to prosperity. He has
admitted that he hesitated before accepting the job when
it was offered to him by outgoing CEO Lee L. Morgan.
Crisis management can drain an executive and take him
away from his family and interests in the community. After
two weeks he accepted, but he told *The New York Times*
soon afterward, "I wish I could believe that things have
hit bottom." An accountant by training, Schaefer is
known as a team player who has good relations with his
fellow executives and subordinates. He has not built a reputation, however, as a dynamic, aggressive leader who
might be expected to be thrust into such a situation. Of
course, his major problem is that he has no control over
the external elements that are most affecting his business.
What is he to do about the value of the dollar, the price of
oil, the state of overseas economies, the cost of foreign

labor, and the expense of servicing the Third World debt?

This is not to say he is completely helpless. He must adapt the company to external conditions as they are now, not as they were in the glorious past. The strongest allies a CEO has in an externally caused crisis are reserves and patience. Cat is rapidly running through its reserves while cutting costs and downsizing to buy time for a better day. Recent weakness in the dollar has aided the company financially, and lower oil prices should help in some Third World markets. But the fundamental problem facing the company is excess production capacity in an industry where very little of it is being retired. This puts intense pressure on prices and a premium on low labor costs, which runs against Cat's past style of high prices and high labor costs.

Like the auto industry, Cat and the rest of the construction equipment makers misunderstood or underestimated the threat from Japan. Cat assumed that quality and service would always triumph over price. "As foreign competitors improved their products, United States producers were getting fat," one industry analyst commented dourly. "During the 1970s they were serving markets that were large and booming and they didn't pay enough attention to costs. That hurt when things changed so devastatingly." The market for the machines manufactured by Caterpillar and its competitors shrank from $21 billion at the peak to $14 billion in 1983, a drop of one-third. Being "excellent" in one set of conditions was not enough when world events changed the rules of economic battle.

CHERNOBYL

Recently we felt the aftereffects of the near meltdown at the Chernobyl generating plant in the Soviet Union. Suddenly all our assumptions about a prolonged oil glut, low-priced commodities, and low inflation in the United States were in question. A single international crisis event thousands of miles away and behind the Iron Curtain touched off the largest one-day drop (to that point) in the Dow Jones Index in history — down nearly 42 points. "The disaster at the Chernobyl Nuclear Generating Plant ... provide[s] proof of just how vulnerable the American and world economy has become to unpredictable shocks," commented Leonard Silk in *The New York Times*. The lesson is clear — adverse international events affect us in ways we find hard to believe. Crises do strike from faraway points. Often we can detect them coming. Rarely can we control them. Yet we must learn to manage through them.

12

Regulation-Deregulation
"The Consummate Crap Game"

IT TOOK US ninety years as a nation (from 1890 to 1980) to impose systematic regulation on business and otherwise establish far-reaching government control over commercial activity. In less than eight years we have completely deregulated some of the most tightly governed of those industries, and the resulting shock has been of crisis proportions. The complex net of laws, rules, administrators, and court rulings was formed when the general public came to accept social controls as a means of curbing real or imagined abuses by business. But the cost was high, the effect chilling, and the results debatable.

Indeed, many studies showed that the major beneficiaries of regulation were not the consumers, who were supposed to be protected, but the regulated industries themselves. Some of them — airlines, for example — maintained a comfortable profitability despite a cost structure that had certainly got out of hand. Protected by the regulatory walls of agencies like the Civil Aeronautics Board, the Federal Aviation Administration, and the International Air Transport Association, the airlines had their profits ensured by restrictions imposed on competition and by prices set by bureaucrats.

Accommodation and Disruption

Businessmen tended to complain about regulation but quickly became comfortable with it; they learned how to play the game the way the regulators wanted. Even the consumers, who were paying the price for the artificial profits and the regulatory structure that supported them, didn't grumble very much. Regulation was a way of life and no one was aware of anything else.

But economists fretted about the waste in the system, and as worldwide competition became keener in the 1970s, successive administrations of both parties in Washington began to listen. Changing technology was also a moving force, particularly in communications. The regulatory structure developed around the turn of the century to manage telephone and telegraph systems looked more and more like a horse and buggy in the era of computerized telecommunications, and it was largely done away with. The deregulatory movement spread, affecting airlines, railroads, trucking, energy, and financial services. Many of the companies were not prepared for the speed and depth of change. Many were prisoners of their old habits and were bewildered by the new environment. For them, deregulation meant a struggle with change of crisis proportions.

WESTERN UNION

For more than a century Western Union had prospered, first as a fast, reliable messenger service, then as a transcontinental telegraph service, and finally as a worldwide provider of telex communications facilities. For much of that time, entry into its core businesses was blocked by regulatory agencies, so it acted like anyone not facing the lash of competition: it allowed its staffs to swell, its costs to increase, its marketing to drift away from the customer, and its labor contracts to grow steadily more restrictive. Realizing that the advent of high-tech communication methods posed a threat to low-skill workers at Western Union, unions had locked in tough job-security provisions that guaranteed any worker with more than five years' seniority at least that long on the company payroll after his or her job had been eliminated, even if no new work could be found. The company was not unaware of the problems posed by technological change and the holes in the regulatory safety net, but it was unable to turn ventures like electronic mail and satellite communications into profits, and its financial position gradually worsened.

When Robert Flanagan became CEO in 1979, he tried diversification on a broad front. He bought a 50 percent interest in Airfone (a venture designed to allow communication between passenger airplanes and the ground) and other interests. All of this added to the company's debt without producing much in the way of earnings. When Curtis-Wright set out on a raid in 1981, Flanagan bought E. F. Johnson, a manufacturer of cellular telephones, which added more debt but fended off Curtis-Wright only for a time.

Two years later, Curtis-Wright's CEO, T. Roland Berner, and two associates won seats on Western Union's board just as the company was initiating Easylink, an electronic mail system that Flanagan was counting on as the product of the future. However, he was hit with a series of misfortunes: writedowns had to be taken for outdated telex equipment; a communications satellite failed to go into the right orbit; and Japanese manufacturers crowded into the cellular telephone market. "As the situation got tighter, Flanagan ran scared politically of Berner and he started retreating and not listening," said a former executive of the company. Berner complained about the high cost of promoting these new products compared with their slim returns and by August 1984 had Flanagan removed. Said one officer, "They tried too many things, and they all came up craps."

Berner took over as top man temporarily and decided to abandon diversification in favor of cost cutting and concentration on Easylink. He put E. F. Johnson up for sale, extracted a 10 percent wage cut from workers and management, and tried to put together a $100 million bank loan to give him enough cash to push the Easylink program. Berner was a tireless worker, often staying at his desk until midnight. Robert Leventhal, a highly regarded management professional who pulls no punches and who succeeded Berner, says it was called "burnout with Berner" in the company. But the banks balked at the plan and canceled their line of credit in what Leventhal calls "the best thing that happened to Western Union," and Berner resigned.

Later, Leventhal was able to persuade the banks to provide funds to get the company through its immediate cash crisis, but it was clear that labor costs were going to have to be trimmed through reductions in the employment rolls, an end to restrictive work practices, and the hiring of lower-cost, part-time workers. The unions were not happy, but with a company that was losing money and staying in business only at the indulgence of the banks, their power was limited.

After a ten-day strike in July and August of 1985, the United Telegraph Workers union gave up its job-security provision, even though the company had indicated that it wanted to get rid of fifteen hundred to two thousand union jobs. "Our goal was not to kill the cow," an unhappy union leader said. In the era of regulation, there would have been no reason for the union to make concessions, since competition was artificially limited. Without that shield, both management and labor were exposed to economic reality, and consumers got the benefit of less expensive, more imaginative communication services. According to Leventhal, the "biggest challenge was driving out the last vestiges of the public utility mentality."

THE AUTO INDUSTRY

The auto industry in the late 1960s was an example of how alternating bouts of regulations and deregulation can cause panic and chaos. The industry was relatively free of regulation through most of its history until the rise of the consumer movement and its most visible hero, Ralph Nader, whose first issue was auto safety. Fifty thousand people were dying each year on the highways (forty-four thousand still are), and Nader convinced people that the product was the problem. He said the auto companies were negligent in designing cars because they did not pay enough attention to the safety of passengers and pedestrians. He caught the attention of the public, particularly after GM made a particularly clumsy attempt to dig up damaging personal information on him and was forced to apologize publicly. With his allies, Nader persuaded Congress to force the auto companies to design safety into their cars and to establish an agency, the National Highway Traffic Safety Administration, to hold their feet to the fire. For fifteen years the agency dutifully cranked out regulations affecting auto design and manufacture, adding hundreds, perhaps thousands, of dollars to the cost of each car. How many lives were saved or injuries avoided by these strictures has never been established. Statistics seem to indicate that the only regulation that did anything to decrease the carnage on the highway was the imposition of the 55-mile-per-hour speed limit, coupled with the reduction in driving resulting from the fuel shortages.

In 1970, the auto companies faced a worsening of their regulatory crisis. Late that year, it was proposed to expand the Clean Air Act by amendments that mandated auto makers to accomplish in five years' time something they didn't yet know how to do — remove 90 percent of the pollution coming out of the exhaust pipes of their cars. As well intentioned as the law was, it created a ridiculous situation. The industry banded together to stop the measure; representatives of all the auto companies, in a rare display of unity, headed for Washington to meet with Senator Edmund Muskie, the principal sponsor of the legislation.

The delegation met Muskie in his properly senatorial office. There was Ed Cole from GM, Lee Iacocca from Ford, John Riccardo from Chrysler, and me. (My boss, Bill Luneberg, despised Washington so much that he refused to make the trip.) Muskie, to our surprise, received us alone, without the usual gaggle of aides that surround senators.

The senator listened quietly as we argued that there was no scientific basis for enacting clean air restrictions as severe as the ones in his bill. He was unmoved by Ed Cole's plea that even if the regulations could be justified, nobody yet had the technology to comply with them. Riccardo was just as ineffective in emphasizing that the cost of meeting the standards would be enormous, and I didn't make much headway with my request for relief for the smallest company in the industry.

Muskie said that he had a study from the Department

of Health, Education, and Welfare showing that carbon monoxide levels on certain street corners in Chicago were too high for the health of senior citizens. "Don't blame me," he said; "go see HEW." It was obvious that he wasn't going to accept any arguments that might interfere with his political plans. A few days later, on Christmas Eve, the emissions standards were passed by the Senate, and Muskie took his bows before a holiday television audience.

This rush of regulation caught the auto industry unprepared; it had failed to recognize the intensity of the social forces at work. The clean air crisis turned out to be huge, and it later compounded many other serious problems — the two oil embargoes, recession, inflation, high interest rates, and Japanese competition. The law pushed the industry into a series of back-to-back crises that lasted for an entire decade.

BRANIFF INTERNATIONAL

Braniff International was an early fatality in the rush of airline deregulation. The Airline Deregulation Act of 1978 was seen as the opportunity of a lifetime by Harding Lawrence, the chairman of Braniff. He was skeptical that federal authorities would stay with a completely free market once some of its problems became obvious and carriers started being pressed financially, so he was determined to expand as quickly as possible while he had the chance. He wanted to change Braniff, then best known for its brightly colored planes and stylishly dressed stewardesses, from a regional carrier to a worldwide force in aviation. If his basic assumption had been correct, maybe his plan would have worked, but Harding Lawrence misread the social signposts. Consequently, what he did now looks like careless abandon.

Braniff had a long history of slow but steady growth

since it was founded in 1928, during the pioneering days of commercial aviation, by Tom Braniff in Tulsa, Oklahoma. It had moved its headquarters to Dallas and flew mainly in the Midwest before commencing flights to South America in 1946. When Harding Lawrence signed on as CEO in 1965, things started to change rapidly. Lawrence had been operations chief at Continental Airlines, where he had developed a reputation for creativity and a fresh outlook. True to form, he said his goal was to transform Braniff into the nation's first all-jet airline. He declared that the era of the plain plane was over and painted his aircraft in bright, eye-catching colors. His slogan was "If you've got it, flaunt it," and his tactics caught the attention of a public accustomed to the conservative marketing approach of the industry. Revenues and profits grew rapidly, jumping 100 percent from 1972 to 1973, and Lawrence was hailed as a "magician" who had found the formula for success in the air. The future looked so bright that in 1977 he began work on a lavish, $70 million headquarters building at Dallas–Fort Worth Airport.

Since he was apparently on a roll, Lawrence decided to double up on his bets when deregulation became a reality. This was just what he was waiting for. He was thinking nationally and internationally, and moved aggressively. What he was doing was paving the way for a major corporate crisis.

Within six months he had the authority to serve 437 of the thirteen hundred new routes made available by deregulation. Braniff inaugurated flights to Europe, Asia, and the Middle East. Nobody else was moving anywhere near this fast. Lawrence bought thirty-one new airliners, including three jumbo 747s, and took out options on forty-four more. The cost: a staggering $925 million.

No one, certainly not the thoroughly intimidated board of directors at Braniff, sought to slow Lawrence's headlong rush. Howard Putnam, who was hired to clean up the mess after Lawrence was deposed, said that "Harding Lawrence was so strong and so believable and so successful that his board just sat there and nodded their heads yes at every decision." He had so much momentum from his earlier successes that no one dared to question his vision of a greater Braniff, worldwide and powerful. Moreover, Lawrence had made sure there would be no sniping from within. "Harding had put in a very political board," Putnam said. "Lots of fellows from Washington, from government jobs, who loved the free passes on Braniff and came to board meetings and sat there and left. Harding went right ahead and did whatever he wanted to do anyway." When things started to go sour, though, most of his hand-picked directors found themselves pressed by other commitments and resigned. Putnam has recalled that a notable exception was Perry Bass, who stayed on and was a great help in the difficult days that followed.

By 1980, Braniff was flying all across the United States as well as to Western Europe, South America, and Asia. But danger signals were sounding; the precrisis period was at hand. Interest rates began to soar to the highest levels since World War II just as the company was taking on huge new debts to expand its fleet; passenger traffic was dropping owing to the recession; and the loss of Iranian oil forced Braniff into the premium-price spot market for fuel to meet its expanded needs. The full crisis hit in the first quarter of 1980, when the airline reported a loss of $22 million. The unexpected reverse came as the company was trying to line up $765 million to pay for the aircraft it had ordered from Boeing. Braniff had planned to raise much of that amount by selling its older planes, but the bottom had dropped out of the market for the narrow-body airliners it was offering, and few takers were to be found.

For the year, the company lost $180 million, and Lawrence lost his job as a result of pressure from worried lenders. He was replaced by John J. Casey, who had been vice chairman and who was successful in getting employees to accept a 10 percent pay cut and convinced lenders to defer Braniff's $653 million debt until February 1982. But the fundamentals of the business were not getting any better, and the firing of the air traffic controllers by President Reagan in August 1981 further diminished the all-important passenger traffic.

Casey went looking for help and fixed on Howard Putnam, who had been highly successful as CEO of Southwest Airlines, a regional carrier that had tripled its revenues and earnings during his tenure. Putnam was brought on as president, but his arrival was much too late; the patient was too sick to be revived. "Braniff was delivered to me DOA," Putnam told my class at Carnegie-Mellon. He was prepared to undertake heroic efforts to breathe life into the corpse. "We told the board that if you are looking for a government bailout, we're not going. If this thing can live on its own, it ought to live. If it can't, it ought to die."

Despite the uncertainty, Putnam went to work. He simplified the fare structure, dropped the "bleeders" (the worst of the money-losing routes), trimmed the payroll, and launched special promotions to drum up traffic. But cash remained woefully short, and in early 1982 Putnam reluctantly began to consider filing for bankruptcy. According to Philip M. Guthrie, Braniff's chief financial officer, survival was a matter of going to work in the morning "and checking to see how much cash was in the drawer." By May 10 the drawer was empty; three days later Braniff was in Chapter 11 and had shut down its operations. It returned to the airways under new ownership in March 1984 in a much reduced fashion, flying to only nineteen American cities out of Dallas–Fort Worth and with only 25 percent of the employees it once had.

* * *

The Braniff message is clear. Harding Lawrence moved too aggressively into the no man's land of deregulation. He risked everything on his reading — which was a misreading — of the societal rules that were bringing about the changes.

Braniff's crash was the most visible in the air traffic field, but deregulation has brought changes throughout the industry, even to such giants as Delta, American, United, and Eastern. Each has come to realize that its corporate cultures and established methods of operation are not suited to the era of freedom, but each is also aware that it cannot change overnight. All shared Lawrence's fear that deregulation might be short-lived and each held back to see what would happen. It is clear now that deregulation is here to stay and that its effects are far-reaching.

But when the rules have been changed fundamentally, under-reaction can be just as dangerous as over-reaction. The trick is to recognize and exploit the inevitable. The lethargy of some of the established carriers allowed low-fare, no-frills airlines to invade their routes, regional carriers to expand, and chartered lines to begin scheduled service. Soon after deregulation, the number of airlines swelled from thirty-six to two hundred, but the total has now shrunk to about a hundred. As a group, the old trunk carriers have suffered from loss of market share, disarray in pricing, high fixed costs, organizational inflexibility, and poor product management. The changes wreaked by deregulation turned out to be permanent after all. The old, regulated way of doing business was abandoned, leaving a group of dinosaurs exposed to a new and competitive environment. Lately, the industry seems to have realized its vulnerability, and realignments are under way to adapt the air travel system to a deregulated environment.

HOME STATE SAVINGS BANK

Karen N. Horn, president of the Federal Reserve Bank of Cleveland, was jolted as she read her newspaper on Monday morning, March 4, 1985. She had good reason to be disturbed by the news that ESM Government Securities had been declared insolvent by the SEC after nine years of fraudulent activity. This threatened ESM's associate, the Home State Savings Bank of Cincinnati, which had major holdings with the failed firm. Banks in trouble usually look to the Fed for help. In fact, shortly after the news media made public the connection between ESM and Home State, long lines of worried depositors began to form at the thrift institutions's teller windows to withdraw their funds, creating a classic "run." By Friday, Home State had shut its doors, cutting off thousands of depositors from access to their savings.

Mrs. Horn, an economist, educator, and a former vice president of the Bank of Boston, was caught off guard, though she was prepared to play the Fed's legal assisting role. It required quick thinking and fast action to step in and assist as only the Federal Reserve can do. She was up to the challenge.

The first clue that Home State was in deep trouble as a result of the ESM failure, she said, came later that day, when an official of the bank called and asked about the procedures for borrowing from the Fed's "discount window." The call was a clear tip-off that Home State's executives thought they might need a lot of money fast and were preparing to turn to the Fed as the lender of last resort. Knowing that a run at Home State was likely, Mrs. Horn also became concerned about the condition of the Ohio Deposit Guarantee Fund, the private insurance fund that supposedly guaranteed the deposits in the seventy state-chartered savings and loan institutions. Federal regulators had not been able to see the books of the fund, but Mrs. Horn estimated correctly that the amount would not be large enough to cover Home State's losses and that the other S and Ls insured by the ODGF were endangered by Home State's problems.

Acting swiftly, Mrs. Horn called in all her examiners and formed crisis teams. They were given instructions to fan out over the state and set up command posts. Hotel rooms with multiple television sets and radios were the order of the day, she said. Every Lincoln Continental available for rent in Ohio was engaged, simply because the cars were equipped with telephones, so the members of the team could keep in touch while moving from place to place. One of the major objectives of the teams was to follow developments in all parts of the state so that the crisis managers would never have to take action on the basis of rumor, but would always have the latest information. By taking this action, the Fed established the only reliable communications system for the Federal Reserve System chairman Paul Volcker in Washington, Governor Richard Celeste, and other public officials who had to decide what actions to take.

Mrs. Horn's agency was alarmed by the Ohio S and L crisis, but it responded well and learned a lot about crisis management in the process. Nevertheless, precrisis warning signals had not been heeded by the regulatory agencies — including the Fed — and the sensing systems that could have headed off the crisis or minimized its effects were not in place. After all, it was no secret that some S and Ls were getting into trouble as a result of deregulation, and in Ohio, ESM's troubles had been flagged before but the warnings went unheeded by the state.

Shortly after the Home State debacle, which precipitated runs across the state and which closed the ODGF-insured institutions, William Isaac, the chairman of the Federal Deposit Insurance Corporation, predicted that "savings and loan associations as we know them today will not exist in a few years." He estimated that the cost of bailing out the troubled thrift system would be over $100 billion.

But Edwin W. Gray, the chairman of the Federal Home Loan Bank Board, the agency that regulates and insures federally chartered S and Ls, did not agree. He claimed that except for a few institutions that were "hopelessly insolvent," the system was sound. Others warned of potential danger. Willard C. Butcher, the chairman of Chase Manhattan Bank, told a meeting of the Business Council at about the same time that "we have the potential for a very serious thrift crisis in this country."

Five months later, in October 1985, Mr. Gray had changed his tune. Testifying before the House Banking Committee, Mr. Gray proposed raising $8.5 billion to bolster the hard-pressed federal insurance fund. Asked to estimate the extent of the problem, Mr. Gray said his agency expected as many as three hundred S and Ls across the nation to fail, with eventual losses of $14 to $15 billion. More than nine hundred were classified as "problem institutions," he said.

The thirty-two hundred S and Ls constitute the second largest financial industry in the nation. How was it that 30 percent of them got into trouble and 10 percent were headed for extinction? The answer is not complicated. A combination of high interest rates and deregulation produced the formula for failure of many in the once tightly supervised industry. With the addition of a little fraud and political influence, you had a recipe for a crisis serious enough to close Ohio's ODGF-insured banks in March 1985. Not since the Great Depression had there been a failure of this magnitude.

*   *   *

Savings and loans started as local thrift associations where working-class families could earn modest returns on investments of their modest savings, amounts that commercial banks were not interested in. They made their money by lending mortgage money, one of the safest bets a banker can make, since a family will hold on to its house to the end in times of financial difficulty and since, in any event, the house will provide collateral for the loan. The system grew to huge proportions, but until recently the basic rules had not changed.

But now investigators were pointing to "poor-quality loans" as the root of the thrifts' problems. As interest rates soared in the late 1970s, the deregulated S and Ls had to pay more and more to keep their deposits — more, in fact, than their mortgages, many of which had low, fixed rates, could earn. They were eager for investments with higher yields even if higher risks were involved. Deregulation gave them the opportunity they sought.

In search of high returns, Home State's managers loaned securities to ESM, a government securities dealer that had lost money almost from the day it started but had been kept afloat by unperfected loans, totaling $200 million, from Home State and another S and L, influenced by Marvin L. Warner, one of Cincinnati's most prominent businessmen.

Warner had spread his wealth liberally, contributing heavily to the campaign of the governor of Ohio, Richard Celeste. He had been rewarded for his fund-raising efforts with the post of ambassador to Switzerland during the Carter administration and had been a member of the Democratic National Committee.

Home State had always operated in a looser regulatory environment than many other S and Ls, because its state charter exempted it from many of the rules governing institutions chartered by the federal government and regulated by the Federal Home Loan Bank Board. Because it could invest in high-yield, risky assets, it could attract depositors by paying them higher interest rates — as long as those assets appeared to be performing. Home State's trading with ESM was in repurchase agreements; that is, Home State bought securities from ESM, which agreed to repurchase them in the future at specified prices. It also made so-called reverse repos, in which it sold securities to ESM, agreeing to repurchase them in the future. These transactions allowed Home State to book quick profits, the cost of which was put off for a time.

State regulators grew alarmed at Home State's exposure to problems at ESM, as early as 1982 calling the S and L's involvement with the firm a matter "of extreme supervisory concern." But these regulators lacked the power to act on their concerns, and the transactions continued. As long as new investors provided a cash flow, ESM stayed afloat, though subsequent investigations disclosed that it had been "hopelessly insolvent" since 1980. When federal authorities finally closed in on ESM, the Home State crisis was at hand. Many investors found that what they had thought of as sound collateral had been pledged on multiple loans and that they were likely to receive only cents on the dollar once the mess was sorted out. Home State alone stood to lose $315 million, according to early accountings. Since the private Ohio Deposit Guarantee Fund amounted to only $130 million, depositors' concern for the safety of their money was well founded, even if the exact amounted in the fund had not been disclosed. Despite borrowings from the Cleveland Fed, Home State could not withstand the run, which drained $150 million in cash in just two days. On March 8, Home State's managers said they would not open for business the following day. The bank was placed into conservatorship by state regulatory authorities, who immediately began to search for a buyer.

* * *

Had the problems been contained at Home State, the whole affair might not have attracted much attention. But depositors at other institutions began worrying about the safety of their funds. Suddenly, lots of people wanted their money back. According to Mrs. Horn, there was a pronounced pattern to the withdrawals; branches of other institutions within sight of Home State offices were hit first. As she remarked, "The banking system operates on confidence," and the sight of the lines at Home State offices eroded the confidence of depositors of the privately insured S and Ls in Ohio. A week after Home State was closed, Governor Celeste was forced to shut down the ODGF-insured banks until a way could be found to restore that confidence.

The solution was legislation that provided a subsidy for an outsider to buy Home State and a requirement that the other state-chartered institutions qualify for federal deposit insurance. Many did so quickly. Others were forced to sell to out-of-state institutions, because no local banks were willing to acquire their assets; that brought interstate banking to Ohio. Though no banks were liquidated, the Ohio episode exposed the weakness of private deposit insurance funds, and problems occurred in other states without the security of federal backing. Indeed, administrators of the federal system became concerned toward the end of the year that its resources would be inadequate and asked Congress to be allowed to assess the sound institutions under its jurisdiction an additional \$8.5 billion to help cover anticipated losses.

The Ohio crisis was accentuated by deregulation, and it had many of the classic characteristics of most business crises. The nonperformance was clear, both on the part of Home State managers, who made the risky investments in search of high returns, and state regulatory authorities, who ignored warnings of questionable practices at ESM.

Federal authorities had raised warning flags about ESM as early as 1980, but never bothered to transmit their concern to the state officials who were supposed to be watching over state-chartered thrifts like Home State. The Cleveland Fed responded well once the crisis happened, but it was the bureaucratic division between agencies, coupled with the easing of regulations on institutions once closely sheltered, that allowed it to occur in the first place.

In April of 1986 the White House approved a plan to provide up to $25 billion to the FSLIC to shutter 461 insolvent thrift units, having exhausted all means to keep them open. Despite the Fed's remarkably good efforts in Ohio, the S and Ls in the U.S. are experiencing the predictable effects ending a poorly managed crisis — radical change.

PART THREE

Dealing with Disruption

13

Thinking Tools for Crisis Management

IT IS TIME for solutions. What can be done to deal with the destructive forces of change? Must we let them run their course, or can we actively manage a crisis? Is it possible to limit the adverse effects? Is it possible to prevent a crisis altogether?

MANAGING CHANGE

First, step back and consider the more general subject of managing change itself. Some regard change as a force that is inevitable and unmanageable, but this is not necessarily the case. Change can be guided, and the pace of it can be quickened or slowed; to influence change, you must anticipate events and move to dominate them.

When we observe slow change coupled with major change, we are comforted by a feeling of *evolution*, the gradual but fundamental altering of the existing structure. Commercial activity has evolved since before the Middle Ages in this manner. Barter gave way to the exchange of goods for money; there were the craftsmen and the guilds; then came mercantilism, capitalism, the Industrial Revolution, social reform, and scientific management. In the 1960s and 1970s, business came to accept the need for a more farsighted outlook, for what was called strategic planning. This move supported the belief that slow and major change can be managed.

Successful strategic planning, however, depends on sound assumptions. It is only when the reasoning behind a plan remains valid over time that the strategy is useful. If the bedrock assumptions prove wrong in the first place or shift in unexpected and unnoticed ways, the plan is not likely to work. Then the situation is ripe for a crisis, because fast and major unanticipated change will follow.

Management of Change

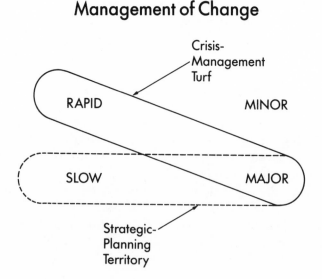

That is the turf of the crisis manager. To date, little formal attention has been devoted to managing a business during periods of instability, and, as a consequence, we have only a few ways to deal with crisis. The most important point, however, is that strategic planning and crisis management are complementary. They coexist comfortably because both deal with the management of change. Crisis management concentrates on those brief moments of instability that must be dealt with first in order to get on with the larger and less time-sensitive job of reaching strategic objectives.

Unmanaged Crisis

In earlier chapters I discussed the unmanaged crisis as it works its way through a company's system like a disease. I described the phases that a company goes through and the likely outcomes.

Most crises begin with chronic but undetected *nonperformance*, and their pace is slow; one thing leads to another. The pace picks up, and then *failure* of devastating dimensions results from the neglect of deep-seated problems. If intervention is still deferred, the ultimate penalty will be *radical change*. For business this means Chapter 11 bankruptcy, Chapter 7 liquidation, or, if the firm still has some valuable assets, perhaps absorption by another company. (In a political environment, a bailout by the government is possible, as happened with Chrysler and Continental Illinois Bank.)

Managed Crisis

This sequence can be altered considerably by a knowledgeable management alert to early signs of trouble and willing to act quickly to minimize the damage. Even though the exact start of a crisis cannot always be forecast with a great deal of precision, it can be anticipated and moderated. The earlier the intervention, the less pain and disruption there will be.

If the crisis is detected early and is aggressively managed all the way, events are likely to unfold in this manner:

Stage	*Sequence*
Precrisis:	Evidence $\longrightarrow$ Acknowledgment $\longrightarrow$ Resolve
Crisis:	Climax $\longrightarrow$ Assessment $\longrightarrow$ Direction
Postcrisis:	Rebuilding $\longrightarrow$ Recovery $\longrightarrow$ Reform

Early warning sensors pick up evidence of repeated nonperformance, and trouble is acknowledged for what it is — a harbinger of deeper difficulty. At that point, the precrisis teams are mobilized and every effort is made to head off or minimize the difficulty.

When the controlled climax arrives, the prevailing attitude should be that of deliberation; the emphasis should be on understanding as much as possible. With this sort of approach, options can be assessed and reasoned orders formulated. It is imperative to come up with a short-term plan to limit damage in the immediate period ahead, often the next couple of days or even hours.

To do so, you don't need reams of information or all of the details; usually only two or three things are crucial. As Harry Gray has put it, "Get what you can and then act."

In the Bhopal incident, the vital unknown in the early hours was *what was going on* halfway around the world. Then, *what help could be provided* to the injured people and *how to get it to the scene* became the essential information. Because Union Carbide had no system in place to supply this vital crisis information, there were damaging delays.

Finally, the postcrisis stage of the fully managed crisis

begins with rebuilding and recovery in the area that has been under siege. It will probably be a baling-wire and Band-Aid job at first, but it is best to get on with it quickly, using whatever means are at hand.

The final step is to adapt the organization to the change that has taken place. Reform, of course, is much less traumatic than *radical change* resulting from an unmanaged crisis; the costs will be far lower and the company will be able to accept the change with a degree of grace. We cannot deny change for long; the trick is to recognize its inevitability and adapt to it in ways that serve the interests of a company's many constituencies.

There is no grade of "perfect" in crisis management — it is a matter of reducing pain and damage — but the results are measurable in big dollar savings and protection of human resources.

CRISIS CLASSIFICATION FACTORS

It is helpful, in understanding a crisis and its effects, to have formal methods by which to classify and identify the forces at work. The four major factors in establishing the classifications are:

- Dimension: The size of the stake at risk
- Control: Your ability to influence the environment
- Time: How much time you have for maneuvering
- Options: The number and quality of your choices

The way in which these factors relate dictates what management tools should be applied. We can plot these factors on a crisis classification grid. Initially we will examine the relationship between the magnitude of the trouble forseen (dimension) and management's ability to influence its environment (control).

Dimension versus Control:
The Classes of Crisis

Two of the zones are especially important. The lower right sector indicates a situation where a great deal is at stake (at 100, the entire company is exposed) and where the management has little or no control of the forces behind the crisis. When a firm faces such a Class A crisis, its existence is threatened. This is where Chrysler was in 1980 and 1981 and where Wheeling-Pittsburgh Steel was in 1985.

The upper right quadrant, the Class B crisis, is also serious, but management retains a measure of control over events. Johnson & Johnson was in this region until it successfully worked its way out of the crises brought on by both episodes of Tylenol capsule poisonings.

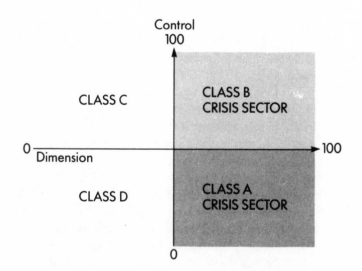

Changing Positions

A company entering a crisis should realize that its situation is fluid. It will move through stages of importance as time goes by. Thus, it might start out in Class C, with a high degree of management control and relatively little danger, pass into Class B, with the stakes rising but management still able to affect its fate, and fall into Class A, where the company is on the line and management can do little to influence the outcome. In fact, this is the sequence that Archie McCardell of International Harvester experienced from 1979 through 1981.

To manage a crisis successfully, it is wise to establish first where you are on the grid. Each position suggests different options. If McCardell had realized that Harvester was moving from a Class C crisis to a Class B, with the

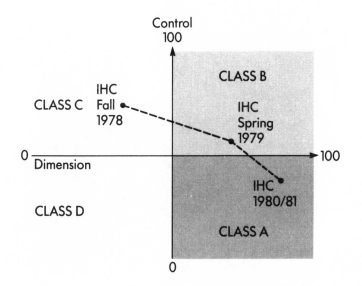

potential of falling into Class A territory, it is likely that he would have changed tactics and found a way to end the destructive labor dispute at Harvester and salvage what he could long before he did.

The Envelope of Executive Concern

Of course, senior management has more concern in some areas of the grid than others. Interest is at a maximum at the 100 point on the dimension axis, because the very existence of the company is in question. What may not be as obvious is that management attention is less important as either the 0 or 100 point is approached on the control line. After all, if a manager has complete control of his environment, there is little to worry about; he can manipulate the crisis as he sees fit. At 0, he has no control at all and may as well go fishing and read about the outcome in the newspapers. The area of serious and urgent management interest is illustrated in the shaded parabola below:

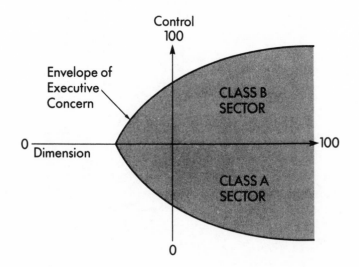

This vital area of management interest is the "envelope of executive concern." A crisis falling within the area warrants management's attention; the skillful use of crisis management tools can have a positive outcome. If a situation is only approaching the boundaries of the envelope, it is time to pay attention and alert the crisis control network. Martin Marietta did just that in 1981, when Tom Pownall formed crisis response teams and enlisted the services of several outside resource organizations, including the investment firm of Kidder Peabody, to defend against an anticipated attack. The measures paid off. It was Kidder Peabody that detected Agee's initial moves months before he struck. "We knew about it in June," Martin Siegel (then an official of the firm) has said. Afraid that he would be exposed or pre-empted, Agee attacked in August, months before he had planned to do so.

The Jaws Zone

Top Management, that is, the CEO and his closest vice presidents, should concentrate their efforts on an even more limited area within the envelope. Realistically, they cannot drop everything each time the corporate ship enters hostile waters — it is there most of the time, anyway — but if it is headed for a dangerous minefield, the captain should know so and focus his energies on getting through undamaged.

Consider the V-shaped "jaws" of the next illustration. It denotes the area of top management involvement when a crisis is detected. Anywhere inside the shaded area of the jaw, the stakes are high and control is insufficient. If the company is in this zone, the CEO should turn his attention from everything else and focus on the crisis at hand. Warren Anderson of Union Carbide did this when

Jaws I

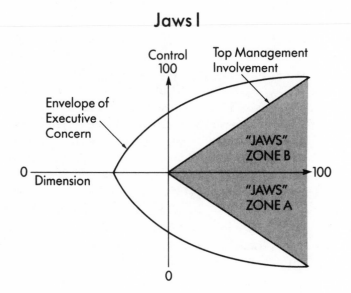

the Bhopal tragedy struck, turning the management of his company over to lieutenants while he and his crisis team concentrated on his Class A "jaws" crisis. He knew that the situation demanded his full attention and that there might be no company left unless he applied all his energies to the crisis. Any executive who has been in this position will tell you the same thing: managing a "jaws-area" crisis is all-consuming and unforgettable. It requires one's full time and undivided attention, to the exclusion of all other matters.

Time versus Options

So far we have dealt with only two of the forces of crisis, *dimension* and *control*. The others, *time* and *options*, are also important. A similar control classification grid can be drawn for these factors:

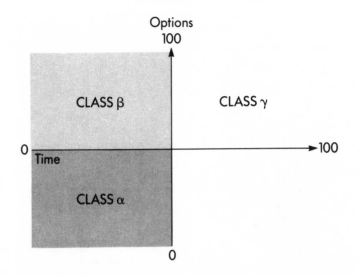

Now we consider how much time we have to react to a crisis (horizontal axis) and what options or courses of action are available (vertical axis). The less time and the fewer the options, the more serious the trouble. Accordingly, the areas of most concern are on the left, and the most serious quadrant is the lower left one, Class Alpha. A Class Beta crisis also is short on time, but there are more options from which to choose.

The Time-Option Jaws

As you might expect, the envelope of executive concern and the jaws are also on the left side of the graph, and the result is a mirror image of what we saw earlier.

A Class Alpha crisis struck the Continental Illinois Bank in 1984. Facing a huge run caused by the collapse of lender confidence, it retreated into the arms of the Federal Deposit Insurance Corporation. It had run out of time and had no other choice.

Jaws II

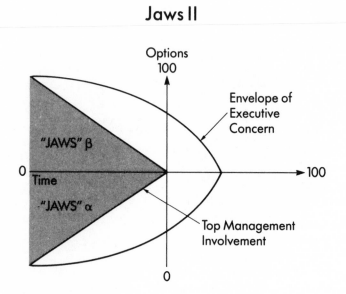

George Baker, then the executive vice president of the bank and top lending officer during the early days of its crisis, said the bank's crisis "was an absolute debacle. I've never seen anything like it. I departed in November 1982 because the next eighteen months would have killed me."

Double Jaws

Of the more visible crises of the last few years, the most memorable and most difficult for those involved were the ones that fell into jaws of both classification grids.

General Public Utilities' crisis with its nuclear power station at Three Mile Island had all the earmarks of both a Class A and a Class Alpha crisis. There was very little time to react, management's options were few, the dimensions of the disaster were potentially enormous, and management had almost no control over its environment. It looked like this:

Double Jeopardy

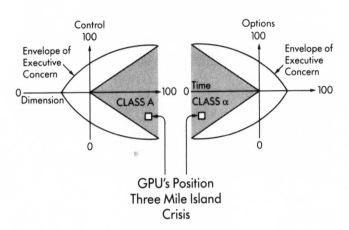

GPU's Position
Three Mile Island
Crisis

If you determine that you are headed for a similar predicament, brace yourself; it's not going to be pleasant. More important, get prepared. There is plenty of work to be done.

Using Thinking Tools

What we have discussed has been designed to help managers identify the gravity of a situation and develop a perspective for dealing with it. By using the framework outlined so far, you will be better able to assess your position when a crisis happens. Decide whether you are facing a managed or unmanaged crisis; determine where you are on the pain curve and in the crisis sequence. Size up your company's standing in terms of the four major crisis factors: *dimension, control, time,* and *options.* Try placing your firm in this context graphically (if only in your mind), and if you are in the jaws of a crisis, face up to the fact.

Once you sense your position, you can move more confidently in taking corrective action.

14

Organizing for Crisis

ANY FIRM can encounter a crisis. Some companies, though, are more crisis-prone than others. The first steps in crisis management are to determine (1) how likely you are to run suddenly into deep trouble, and (2) how well prepared you are to deal with it.

Sometimes entire industries teeter on the edge of crisis because the winds of change are blowing hard and their leaders haven't taken notice or made preparations. Steel, autos, textiles, chemicals, mining, trucking, and airlines are just a few of the sectors that have been caught unprepared for major structural change. For the auto industry, it took the entire decade of the 1960s to convince the key players that consumerism was a real force in the economy, that safety and environmental concerns were permanent, that quality standards were rising, and that the Japanese were going to set a new standard for competition. With all those changes going on at once, it is not surprising that the industry reeled from one crisis to another for ten years.

The first move in any assessment of crisis is examining where your industry stands in the business environment. Should you conclude that change is on the way, determine whether you or your competitors are leading or falling behind. If you are lagging, even though your current cash flow is ample, be aware that you are headed for a crisis. There is no need to be fatalistic if you have time and resources available for action. But act you must; things will only deteriorate from this point.

A good way to keep track of changes outside your company is to establish special sensors — outsiders whom you trust to observe the scene and tell you of changes that will affect your future. A company heavily dependent on overseas markets should assemble an international advisory board of well-placed people in those markets. Forget titles and big names; seek out those who are active every day in their markets: traders, manufacturers, or financiers who are involved in commercial dealings relevant to your business. Similar panels can be set up to help you keep abreast of changes in other parts of your world. Some banks and multinational firms have these groups in place already.

In many instances, the forces at work externally are not as difficult to assess as those inside your own company. So much filtering of information and "ass covering" goes on within any large organization that the beginnings of a crisis can easily go undetected.

THE CRISIS AUDIT

A company that has a history of crises or is in an industry being rocked by major change should perform a crisis audit on itself. An even better approach is to bring in an outsider to do the job, thus ensuring objectivity and candor.

Crisis Susceptibility Audits

The first part of a crisis audit should address itself to exposing the kinds of crises your firm is likely to face. General Motors doesn't need to spend much time preparing for a hostile takeover, but it has had some severe confrontations with government regulators, sudden market shifts, and adverse international events.

Each area of the business should be closely examined for its vulnerability to unexpected, rapid change. After you assess the possible exposures, rank the nine crisis types outlined in Part II in their order of concern for your company and use that ranking to assign priorities to your resources. A brief example of an audit summary is on page 220.

This hypothetical metals company will apply its energies to its immediate problems with cash and labor. When those preparations are completed, it should turn to its potential difficulties with public perception and management succession. Most often it is necessary to address potential problems in this sequential fashion. It is the rare organization that can prepare for more than two crises at a time.

Crisis Capability Audits

However the crisis audit is performed, Part II should answer three questions relating to your firm's ability to deal with sudden disruption:

1. To what extent can your organization *detect* a crisis at an early stage?
2. How well will it *manage* a crisis if one occurs?
3. To what degree will it *benefit* from a crisis after it has passed?

Crisis Susceptibility Audit Summary

American Metals Corporation, Inc.

(Producer of basic and finished metal products)

Crisis type	Vulnerability	Priority	Action
Cash	High and immediate	Top (1)	Full attention
Industrial relations	High and immediate	Top (1)	Full attention
Public perception	Serious and current	High (2)	Maintain top awareness
Top management succession	Serious and current	High (2)	Maintain awareness
Hostile takeover	Unlikely but possible	Moderate (3)	Monitor
Sudden market shift	Remote	Low (4)	None
Adverse international event	Remote	Low (4)	None
Regulation and deregulation	None	None (5)	None
Product failure	None	None (5)	None

The precise design of the audit is not particularly important if it gives you the answers to these questions. Here, though, are some initial questions to ask in developing a crisis capability audit.

Detecting crisis at an early stage

- Do you have early warning sensors?
- Are crisis responsibilities clear?
- Is management open to surprise and criticism?
- Does bad news travel upward easily in your company?
- Are there enough mature and talented people to withstand the sting of exposed failure?

Managing a crisis when it hits

- Has a crisis team been selected and trained?
- Is your organization design flexible and open?
- Are resources marshaled to cope with adversity?
- Is outside help lined up and available on short notice?
- Are instructions and assignments clear, current, and rehearsed?

Benefiting from a crisis

- Does change happen easily in your organization?
- Do you have the desire to improve and grow?
- Are you capable of accepting new ways?

CRISIS TEAMS

Notice the emphasis in the crisis capability audit on having a crisis team. Medicine has demonstrated that it is the most important organizational device we have for coping with crisis. The right people, properly trained, must be in a good position to manage a crisis when it hits.

The crisis team is not a new concept. Some companies

misuse the term to describe their security forces; others apply it loosely to committees that are set up for any important purpose. A few are advanced enough in their thinking to refer to their full-time crisis teams, trained and prepared for special eventualities.

United Technologies applied the term *crisis team* to ad hoc groups that Harry Gray selected to help him whenever he was in trouble. I recommend this approach for crises that fall into the "unthinkable" category because of its flexibility. When I was a CEO, my inclination was to take personal charge of a major unforeseen problem and tailor the crisis team to the nature of the problem. If the surprise difficulty was less severe, I would still select a team, but would hand over its leadership to a trusted senior officer.

It often makes sense, particularly for "thinkable" crises and for certain crisis-prone companies, to have permanent crisis management teams. Chemical, pharmaceutical, aerospace, and airline companies know that every risk cannot be designed out of their products. They should therefore prepare for the "thinkable" but horrifying possibilities their customers could face, and they should also prepare for the "unthinkable" problems that somehow seem to arise.

The teams should be composed of people who are especially suited to getting the job done. They should have frequent contact, be in close proximity, and work well together. Each member should be prepared to forgo his normal routine and outside interests during a crisis. And all should be very well compensated for performing "combat duty."

Whether the choice is for ad hoc crisis management teams or a more institutionalized approach, the people involved should represent and possess creativity, knowledge, power, and perspective.

Creativity

The most creative senior executive in the company who can take pressure and will accept the assignment should be chosen for the group. He can be the most important team member you have. This is the person who will sketch out the scenarios, think the unthinkable, and offer options for dealing with tough problems. However, he must not infect the rest of the organization with his thinking, particularly the possible negative outcomes.

Knowledge

Another member is the person who knows how the business really works. He need not be a strategist or a profound thinker, but he should have wide experience. He should know where the skeletons are hidden, and his contacts throughout the company should be among the best. He will be the primary source of intelligence and the chief assessor of the threat, sizing up the magnitude of trouble and estimating its potential impact. Often, this person is the chief operating officer.

Power

When the time comes to act, this person will have authority and resources. He will probably be the senior member of the team, the one who sets up the command center and serves as the communications nexus. At some companies this will be the CEO, but many CEOs are ill suited to the task, and a surrogate must be selected. If the CEO himself is part of the problem — as in a management succession crisis — it is up to the board or owners to provide guidelines for the crisis team.

Perspective

No matter how hard we try, we cannot get on the other side of the mirror. Only somebody from the outside can tell you how you look to others. And since public perception is so important in many crises, somebody from outside the organization should be available to the crisis team. The best choice is one who, though unconnected to your company, is familiar with your business or industry and may have faced some of the same problems. A frank view and a willingness to express it are essential. A consultant can play this role, but be sure he is experienced, up to date, and isn't in it just for the money.

Crisis-Team Training

Crisis teams must be trained; raw talent will not suffice. Simulations will help a team learn how to recognize a crisis, what actions are appropriate, how to develop options, assess time, consider dimensions, and judge control. Since there are no formal training centers to teach these skills (public relations firms excepted), it will be necessary to design your own program or have a nearby university or consulting firm do it for you. If nothing else, the team should be intimately familiar with the crises other companies have gone through; just digging into the facts and strategies of others who have dealt with similar circumstances will give the team important background information to draw on.

Using Professionals

Team members should know in advance that when special talents are required, outside experts, such as takeover lawyers, public relations professionals, political pundits, international affairs advisers, investment bankers, and so forth, are available. These people are no substitute for management dedication, but they can be of enormous assistance when time is short and internal talent is limited. Get them lined up in advance and have them on call; get to know one another. A professional who is ready to go when trouble hits suddenly will be of enormous assistance.

A word of caution: outside professionals come with their own biases. Don't expect them to see your crisis as you do. Some, in fact, have a stake in crisis; they thrive on it, promote it. Look for these biases when you approach them. Be certain that the people and organizations you hire really want to solve your problem, not just run up a fat fee. In fact, this is a proper place for contingency fees. Set up a payment schedule that rewards performance. Crisis consultants should be paid for results, not hours. (They should also be paid well and promptly.) If one does not measure up, cut him off immediately. Bill Agee says he suffered too long with inadequate investment bankers, public relations counselors, and corporate lawyers and that their failings in large part doomed his attack on Martin Marietta.

SET UP A CRISIS CENTER

In some corporate cultures, it is useful to set up a special place for a crisis to happen. A crisis control center can be good for focusing activity. It should be accessible, but not a team member's office, and it should be entirely dedicated to crisis management, sealed off from the day-to-day activities of the organization. Special telephones, computer terminals, and televisions should be installed as needed. Blackboards, diagrams of installations, pictures of key people, organization charts, and information on products and processes should be readily available.

Permanently on file at the crisis center should be all contingency plans, scenarios, and emergency procedure instructions that have been developed in advance. The addresses and telephone numbers of major players should be on hand, as should information on outside resources.

The crisis center should be used during precrisis for:

1. Intelligence gathering
2. Threat assessment
3. Scenario development and testing
4. Episode investigation
5. Simulation training

In the postcrisis period, it should be used for:

1. Scenario reconstruction
2. Early warning system design
3. New strategy development

But the most active period at the crisis control center will be during the crisis itself. Team members will assemble there and probably stay for the duration of the event. The post will be used for:

1. Fact gathering
2. Situation evaluation
3. Options assessment
4. Action selection
5. Issuance of instructions
6. Progress monitoring

Even smaller organizations may wish to set aside a special place for a crisis team to ensure that there will be full concentration during critical periods. Having such a facility will promote prompt and responsible reactions to disruption. Normal office settings are filled with distractions and should be saved as places of refuge from the high pressure of the crisis center.

15

Managing a Crisis

CRISES HAVE common elements, which means that there are some fundamental approaches to understanding and dealing with them. This does not mean they are all alike. To the contrary, each type of crisis has its unique characteristics. Just because you understand the general nature, usual structure, and expected outcome of a crisis, you do not necessarily have the tools to manage it effectively. Each of the nine major types of crises that affect business today requires a tailored approach. What follows are some practical guidelines drawn from my experience and the thoughts of some of the best minds in the field today.

Think about the person inserted at the climax, when the chaos is at its worst. Someone thrust in at this point will not have the advantage of the warm-up of the pre-crisis period, will have no advance warning or preparations in place to minimize the effects of the unmanaged crisis. Suddenly it is upon him and must be dealt with.

This happens so often that it is useful to examine the worst possibilities and offer some suggestions for solutions.

CASH CRISIS

Your company is in the advanced stages of a financial crisis: cash is scarce, outside sources of funds have dried up, internal ones seem inadequate to cover current needs, lenders are nervous, and credit agreements are close to default. Employees are frightened and suppliers are worried about not getting paid. Members of the board of directors are looking for reasons to resign. What do you do now?

Take Control of Cash

Absolutely the first thing to do is make love to your cash. Find it, protect it, enhance it, and control its flow. Do so personally. Uncover pools of it that have not been tapped; look into the payment terms that have been extended to customers and shorten them. Check especially into foreign operations or favored customers who have got your salespeople to agree to sweet terms; simply cutting their payment terms to you from sixty to thirty days will buy a month's cash.

Take the opposite approach with suppliers. Tell them bluntly where things stand and lengthen your payment terms to them from fifteen to, say, forty-five days. This buys another month's respite.

Dig deep into the corporate structure to find other sources of cash. Look for worthwhile but nonessential assets that can be sold. Slow or stop cash-draining programs. Drop frills, such as first-class travel or club memberships, for symbolic reasons.

Insist that the cash position be monitored continuously and the fresh information placed on your desk. Know how much cash is on hand at all times, how much will be spent soon, and what the remaining level will be. Project that level for ten to thirty days and watch it daily. Be on top of the situation personally and be prepared to take action if cash starts to slip out of control.

Listen Hard

The main purpose of seizing control of cash is to buy time. Once you've done that, your next step is to find the bleeders — the cash-consuming, nonessential operations — as well as the people who will be able to help you. This sort of reconnaissance is especially important if you are new to the scene. Take the time to make a thorough review.

You will be under intense pressure to "do something" — to fix the crisis. Resist the pressure to take premature action. Talk to your people individually to find the crisis heroes, the handful of managers who have a clear understanding of the situation, see it the way you do, and can deal with any ambiguity involved. After you find them, tell them what you expect and lean on them hard.

During this period you will discover where you are bleeding the worst. Usually there are only a few grievous wounds, but this is the information you must obtain from your crisis team. Identify the problems, set up your own triage, and solicit advice on what can be done to heal the salvageable.

Stop the Hemorrhaging

Go after the two or three worst cash drains with a vengeance — be merciless in shutting them. It won't be easy. You will hear all sorts of objections, from "It's a tradition" to "We've invested millions in it." Don't listen. Close the cash drains to buy more time and the opportunity to rebuild the business.

Find the Positives

As you address the worst problems, keep a sharp eye out for opportunities. Sometimes, when the underbrush has been stripped away, it becomes clear that you have a great core business that should be enhanced. At other times it becomes obvious that you have some unrecognized cash producers to promote. (Think in terms of cash and only cash. Reporting profits is not important at this stage — cash is what keeps you alive.) Once again, pick only a few winners to support immediately. You haven't got the time or energy to devote to a complex, multifaceted program. Get behind a few projects and put your resources to work.

Make a Plan

Now is the time for a short-range plan. For starters, look forward ninety days. Forget strategic concerns; figure out how you are going to make it to the end of this month and, when you get there, the next one and the next. If you survive the ninety days, try it again. Little by little, as you accomplish your plans, you will prove your staying power, confounding those who expect to write you off. Once things are partially stabilized, lay out a six-month program and prepare to sell it.

Raise New Cash

With your six-month plan in hand, look for new sources of cash. Wherever you go, your business plan will be crucial: it must be realistic and understated. Local lending institutions will be a hard sell; you may have to pledge assets or sacrifice some independence. Capital may be available if your plan is convincing, but be prepared to relinquish some control.

An investment banker who is familiar with your operations and plans can be useful in connecting you with a source of funds — for a hefty fee. Nevertheless, this could be a good investment.

Raising new cash is the most vital step to moving ahead. Do it well, and you have a new lease on life; your failure to do so will mean more day-to-day scrounging around just trying to ensure survival. Worse than that, the company will be shaken by even minor shocks and completely thrown by harder ones.

Re-establish Credibility

If you have progressed through the preceding steps, you are beginning to pick up some momentum. The worst is actually behind you, but now you have to start shedding the "loser" image. First, meet your obligations as scheduled; carry through with your business plan.

Then start projecting yourself as one who has accomplished a turnaround. Take the message to your public, and don't be bashful about disclosing your return to the world of business as a viable competitor.

Improve Attitudes

Project your company as a survivor to your own employees as well as to stockholders, suppliers, lenders, and the media. Develop a winner's attitude in public. Speak freely about what you have been through; proclaim your company as a new, reborn outfit with a mission and a vision of the future.

Show a Profit

The crowning step will be the day when you can report a small, honest profit. Of course, it can't be a one-time occurrence; it will have to be followed by other such reports.

But it will mark the time when you can relax your concentration on cash and begin to plan for periods longer than ninety days or six months.

Among the better-known companies that have followed this path back from the brink of extinction are Chrysler, Wickes, International Harvester (Navistar), Braniff, and Continental Airlines. A more recent example is Wheeling-Pittsburgh Steel. "Red" Scott, a well-known turnaround specialist from San Diego, has been applying this thinking to small firms for years.

Managing a cash crisis is an exercise in buying time — enough time to remedy the problems that brought the company to its knees. The fundamental assumption is that the company was worth saving, because it had a product or service of economic value.

PUBLIC PERCEPTION CRISIS

All of a sudden your company is in the spotlight. You have suddenly become the focus of the media's attention, and your methods of doing business are under their microscope. Practices that have gone unchallenged for years are being questioned. The tone is hostile, and officers and directors are on the defensive. Phones ring at all hours and reporters demand interviews and more information. The national press — *The New York Times, The Wall Street Journal*, and *The Washington Post* — along with the television networks, can't wait for carefully considered reports. They'll go with what they have, even if it is only part of the story. How should you react?

Quickly Take Charge

Time is the most important factor. The first act of a crisis manager must be to assign himself as the major absorber of information and dispenser of instructions. Don't delegate this task. Let everybody inside the organization know who you are. Tell them you want to know everything possible as soon as possible. Be accessible to anyone with useful information. Go to the trouble spot and stay there as long as you need to grasp the implications of what has happened. Set up a command post, open lines of communication, and monitor the media for the latest developments. Above all, get on top of the situation and be in a position to seize control quickly.

Pinpoint the Perception Problem

Reconstruct the events into some coherent pattern. Track down those leading up to the problem, and find out who is involved with them and why. Identify your "influentials" and learn their motivations. Influential parties are usually small groups who stand to gain from damaging your firm, but there are also influentials who have much to lose. Call on them for assistance as your response gets under way. Do a quick and dirty telephone sampling to assess the intensity of feeling among those affected. You may be surprised to find that the public's interest is a lot less than the media attention would suggest — or a lot more. You must know which before you can take action.

You will also need to identify the salient facts. Just what is at issue? What specific aspect of your operation or product is offensive? And why has it suddenly jumped into prominence?

Get Another Opinion

You can't possibly see yourself the way others see you, so bring in a trusted outsider to provide some perspective. The choice may be a professional public relations firm or simply a wise old head whose judgment you respect. Keep this person, or people, close at hand throughout the crisis period. You will get the outside view of your company you need — and something of a conscience.

Construct Your Best Case

No matter what terrible event has taken place, there is still "your story," a reconstruction of the facts and an interpretation of them from the company's point of view. When you relate it, be sure to give the background information revealing important but often overlooked prior events that help explain the current conditions. You must be honest, factual, concerned, and willing to accept whatever blame rightfully attaches to the company.

Whenever the public at large is involved, the most important thing is to protect your credibility. With it, you can recover; without it, you are in for lasting damage.

Cage Your Lawyers

Learn from your legal counsel where the danger points are, and understand your exposure to litigation. Develop a sense of limits on what can be said and done and what words or acts should be carefully avoided. *Do not overreact to the legal concerns!* Most public perception battles are lost by overzealous protection of legal positions. This stance produces the corporate stone wall, which makes even a sincere, concerned management look ignorant, indifferent, and probably guilty.

Communicate

Make contact with all important segments of your public. Tell them what you can. Assure them that you will stay in touch. Encourage them to phone if they are worried or have useful information to pass on.

Establish a Spokesman

Select one person to meet with the media and the public; avoid the contradictions that will inevitably creep in if there are too many voices. Find someone who can tell your story in the most convincing way and make it clear that this is the person outsiders are to query.

Being the spokesman is no easy task. A cool, informed, unflappable person is required, and it won't hurt if he or she looks the part as well. On some occasions it should be the CEO, but he may not be suited to the task. A better choice will probably be a senior executive who has dealt frequently with the media, knows the subject matter thoroughly, and can articulate the company's story. He should be tough-minded as well as affable — the media can sense a pushover.

Accommodate the Media

Develop rapport with the journalists assigned to the story. Designate places and times to go over breaking news, and keep telling your story. Encourage the press to bring you information for comment; often reporters dig up news and uncover relationships faster and more accurately than any other people available to management.

On the other hand, don't be bullied. There is no reason to take abuse from ill-mannered journalists. If you are ambushed by a surprise interview designed to rattle you, make your distaste clear and cut short the meeting. Remember, you are the one in control. You have information to dispense, and the media want what you have. Stay closer to the journalists who will fairly report your position.

Tell Your Story

Make your case with your public. Start early and repeat your story as often as necessary to be sure it is being heard. Be consistent — don't be diverted by speculation. If important information necessary to reach final conclusions is lacking, say so. Then quickly add that your staff is investigating to find out what is needed. Do not accept hypothetical cases; a premature conclusion that is later refuted by the facts is hard to live down.

Improve your story as you learn more; keep it current. If unfavorable developments force you to modify it, do so and explain why. No one blames a company that appears to be keeping an open mind and is responding to new information.

One more point: the day of "no comment" is past. With the public as informed as it is today, those words are interpreted as a confession of guilt. Avoid them.

Fix the Problem and Get Satan Behind You

Whatever it was that set off the public perception crisis must be resolved quickly. Letting too much time elapse between the start of a problem and its resolution will damage a company's reputation, even if it is not at fault. This is not a case of "all's well that ends well"; once a company has had prolonged exposure to negative publicity, the chances of its fully recovering its former esteem diminish. So conclude the matter quickly, before the public, convinced that you are no good, moves on to something else.

A good example of a company that followed these ten steps in dealing with a public perception crisis is Johnson & Johnson with the Tylenol poisonings. The ones who have not are too numerous to mention.

SUDDEN MARKET SHIFT OR PRODUCT FAILURE

Sales are plummeting and there's a strange negative attitude toward your product in the market. Profit hopes have been dashed. Salesmen are clamoring for more promotion money and pricing concessions to clean out excess stock. Production people are bracing for cutbacks and layoffs. Financial people want to cut budgets to limit losses and protect the balance sheet. What should you do?

Quiz Your Customers

Start at the end. Your customers know what is wrong; have them tell you what is going on. Go into the marketplace and find out what your users have to say. Hire a professional market research firm to frame the right questions and design the market samples.

Use focus groups to quiz customers for deeper attitudes that might remain hidden in more structured questioning. Get into the market yourself, and send your executives and salespeople into the field to get a feel for the market. Compare what they find with the more formal results of the surveys and focus groups.

Find the Problem

Gather the information as it starts trickling in and formulate your ideas. Make a first hypothesis and test it against later data. If the research appears headed in a fruitless direction, change its course. If you pick up a scent, follow the trail.

Even if you have a tentative conclusion, don't act until you are reasonably certain that you know the culprit. Keep testing your theses until you run out of time. Remember, you are trying to figure out whether you are selling a product that:

1. has a design flaw and does not measure up to its planned specifications;
2. is satisfactorily engineered but is not being well received because of inadequate marketing efforts;
3. is well designed and marketed, but is not in tune with current tastes, desires, and needs;
4. or suffers from some combination of these three.

Respond

Knowing the reason for a sales collapse is essential if you are to develop an adequate response. If there is a future for the product, decide what you are willing to spend to re-establish it and how much time you have to do that. If a product's day in the market is done, kill it fast. This fatal conclusion, unfortunately, seldom is anything but a last resort. Pride and an excessive need for success in all undertakings can delay management's cutting losses until they are so large that there is no alternative. That is why some product lines tend to become heavy and cumbersome. It takes a crisis to thin them down.

Adjust Production

No matter what the cause of the sales collapse or the planned response, you must adjust output until the problem has been treated. Don't believe the people — still mired in the denial phase — who argue that you can "buy your way" out of the problem with promotion money. It may be that sales will respond temporarily to incentives, but more often those expensive programs just borrow from future sales.

The sooner you balance production with sales, the faster your inventory will drop and cash will be released. Customers know when you are bloated; they will squeeze you on prices until your stock is back in shape.

Revise the Numbers

Now it is vital to step back and take a hard look at the new realities in the numbers. Your projections suffer; a collapse in sales can put your reserves under pressure; your obligations to lenders can become a more critical issue.

Be conservative in your financial forecasts. This will force economies on old budgets and even prompt some fresh thinking. A cash crisis could complicate the situation. Let your people know what's coming. Notify lenders and creditors of the revised outlook. Advise both of your intentions.

Fix the Problem

If you find that your product design is deficient, the theoretical choices are simple. Redesign it or retire it. Of course, doing the former assumes that your product design people have found a solution and that marketing agrees. Salespeople will have to assure you that the market still exists, and the financial staff must agree that you can afford the cost of recovery. If you are given all green lights, launch the product again. The Japanese car companies did so after their initial failures, and the public bought their product.

If inadequate marketing is the problem, you will have to search for a new approach. It's comforting to know that you still have an attractive product; it's a major challenge, however, to revive a failed marketing effort. A simple message change, of course, can be accomplished with the help of your advertising agency.

But strengthening a distribution system that is too weak or unable to finance and service your product line is another matter. This problem takes years to remedy, unless you go the way of a buyout or a merger with another company in the field.

Your troubles are also large if the market has shifted from your product. Very little can be done to salvage even a good product if customers have lost interest. Your best course is a "profitable retreat," in which you cease production, sell what inventory remains for whatever you can get, and turn your attention to other opportunities. This does not always mean entirely abandoning your position in a market, especially if you were the market leader. Just lie low for a while and invest carefully during the downturn if you expect the market to swing back in your direction in the future.

Return

When the timing appears right, move back into the market with your redesigned product and improved marketing program. Win back your customers. Invade your competitors' territory at their weak spots.

When you return, be committed. Put up the resources needed to do the job. Remember, returning is harder than starting out! You have adversity to overcome; you are saying "Forget the past — look at me now." The buying public will be forgiving if the quality is there and if you communicate well. Ask Lee Iacocca.

Don't get carried away by initial success. Increase production slowly. Stay a little bit short. Err on the side of lost sales due to short stocks and let demand push up your output. You are coming back; run lean and protect your prices.

But if you have come back successfully, don't be bashful. Proclaim it! Tell the world that you are back and successful. Success is contagious.

TOP MANAGEMENT SUCCESSION

The chief executive will not retire. Even though he is past the normal retirement age, he remains vigorous, healthy, full of ideas, and produces good results. He is not over the hill by any means — but he's wrong for the future.

For years vice presidents and other senior people have waited and worked hard. Unless they get deserved advancement and recognition, they will go elsewhere. Even though the company is prosperous, it is in need of new vision, something closer to modern times. Your fellow board members have been reluctant to raise the subject. How can the succession process be activated?

Smoke Out the Hidden Agenda

Treat this situation tenderly. It requires a skillful mix of compassion, respect, and resolve. It is a job for outside directors who have courage and are immune or indifferent to retaliation. They have to uncover what the CEO is really up to. Chances are he likes the job and its perks, has limited outside interests, and wants to hang on as long as he can. It is his life. It may not be gentlemanly to say that he enjoys power and his ability to exercise it over others, but this is a big attraction of the top job, and it can be addictive.

Someone, perhaps an esteemed colleague of the CEO, must be assigned to probe his inner feelings. No delegation or committee will get as far. Whatever his motive for hanging on — satisfaction, pride, power, or just the fear of a strange new life — it must be brought to the surface and dealt with. This gets you to the next step: When does he plan to step aside and start the succession process? If it is not any time soon, it is up to you to unhorse him — gently and gracefully if possible.

Assess Your Options

If your CEO wants to stay on just a little while longer, not much harm will come of that. But if he wants another year until his new home is completed in La Jolla, don't wait. Appoint him chairman of the executive committee or make him chairman emeritus. Don't hold up progress because the incumbent wants to follow his own personal program. Devise a plan that takes his needs into account, but get him moving.

The more serious problem arises when a successful CEO has no intentions of leaving. If you discover this is the case, prepare for a battle. But try to prevent one. Usually this problem co-exists with another: there is no good heir apparent in place. He was eliminated before he could become a threat.

Now the situation calls for concerted action. Outside directors must be united and determined to proceed. Discord at this juncture will break the board into armed camps; no one will be able to act decisively.

Shelve the Boss

A logical, considerate series of moves should be planned. If a search is required, time will be needed, so allow for it. Of course, an outside contender will bring with him a measure of uncertainty. Executive search firms have a spotty record on CEOs, but if no one insider measures up, by all means look for the right person, wherever he may be.

Incidentally, it is a mistake to set up multiple succession candidates in a public scramble for the top job. This is a bad habit of some outgoing CEOs embarking on one last ego trip.

If you are involved in getting rid of a reluctant CEO, pick a time and make it a clean break. Don't permit someone who didn't want to give up power to hang around and harass his successor. In this instance, "when you're done, you're done" — out the door and off the board.

Announce the Successor

After the decision has been made, elect the new CEO and announce any moves that will accompany his accession. Do this swiftly; leaks can cause trouble. The announcement should include a clear statement of why the new person has been chosen and why the change is being made now. It should fit with your stated objectives for the future and avoid recriminations about the past.

The announcement is important. It locks in the plan and eliminates ambiguity. If the former CEO had any thoughts about hanging on, this ends them. From now on he is a lame duck. Once that is clear, he should be eager to go for the sake of his own pride.

Observe and Support the Successor

There is no training course or proving ground for a top executive better than being on the job. Until he is there, there is no assurance that a person can handle the power, hold on to his integrity under pressure, and deal with the loneliness. Thus, it's important for you to rally to his side and enhance his prospects of success. At the same time, you can observe his progress.

Enforce the Exit

Occasionally the outgoing boss tries to remain, announcement or no. In a publicly held company, this can result in a national display of disarray. The board must act. A gentle reminder of the golden handshake or a quiet word concerning retirement perks may be necessary to end disputes like this.

INDUSTRIAL RELATIONS CRISIS

Your employees are on strike; they walked out two months earlier, when the old contract expired. Negotiations collapsed after your final offer was refused, and no new meetings have been scheduled. Meanwhile, inventories have been exhausted and your customers are being wooed by competitors. Cash is running low. The top leadership of the union is unsympathetic with your company's predicament and cannot win a ratification vote with a contract anything like the last proposal. What now?

Size Up the Climate

The first thing a new labor crisis manager needs is a clear picture of the facts and the emotional state of the striking employees. Assemble the numbers — current wage and benefit levels, their history, competitors' agreements, what the last company offer was, and precisely how far off it was from the union's demands. To end the walkout you are going to have to find some way to bridge that monetary gap. You will also need the same information for the noneconomic parts of the contract, such as work rules, grievances, representation, overtime, and so forth.

Learn about the political forces at work in the union and become familiar with the power structure behind the strike. Get close to your operating people to learn their thoughts; see whether you can tap the sentiments of the rank and file. You need to know all these things besides the formally stated bargaining positions. Be alert to possible rancor between the bargaining teams and do whatever you can to reduce tension.

Open Up Dialogue

Hold your own meeting, avoiding publicity, with union leaders to demonstrate your willingness to bargain. This will also allow you to assess their attitudes and position at first hand. Find out what pressures they are under. How strong is their resolve and how deep their hostility?

Explain the company's objectives. Emphasize that the workers' future is tied to the company's success. Tell them you want to start negotiations again and that you hope to keep communications open while you both work on devising a settlement. You are their last hope of an early settlement — make this quite clear.

Be sure to state a strong case for keeping the company competitive so that there will be jobs left to discuss in the future. Build credibility with the union leaders by being respectful of their needs and bargaining posture. Make no concessions, but look for common ground. Prepare the union leaders for your return visits.

Isolate the Essentials

Once you have gathered the facts, gotten to know the people and their attitudes, and opened up lines of communication, it is time to fashion the elements of a settlement.

Isolate the issues that divide the two sides and identify those which are vital to an agreement. Put in terms of dollars the offers that may solve the key problems. Can you tolerate the cost for the life of the contract? Perhaps you can't hope to be as efficient as your competitors right away, desirable as that may be; perhaps it is more important to stay alive. But it is also important to know how far you are from the desired goal and to prepare for the next battle. Highlighting the gap with competitors will help sell your offer.

Since noneconomic issues are even more difficult to negotiate than money, concentrate on the few that are vital to you now and leave the others for another day. Remember, it took years to build in all those inefficiencies; unless you have an enormous war chest, you won't get rid of them all in one round of negotiations. The economic battleground is strewn with the corpses of those who tried and failed.

Finally, take a hard look at your negotiating team. If there are bad chemistry problems, change a few assignments to reduce the emotional heat. Increase the roles of those members of the team better able to get results.

Construct an Offer

Construct your new offer. Package the economics you can tolerate with the noneconomic gains you realistically can hope for. If the price of peace is going to be high and a recession is imminent, seek a short-term agreement; your chances of doing better next year will be improved. Maintain a flexible attitude toward the elements of the package, but never lose track of the numbers you need and the negotiating room available. Keep the number of "dealbreaker" items to a minimum. Make sure the union knows what yours are, and be certain you know theirs.

Resume Negotiations

Test the offer quietly and in general terms with the union before scheduling a formal meeting. Get an advance sense of how it will be received. At this point it would be foolish to present something that is going to be rejected out of hand. Don't expect any commitments; you just want some idea of attitude and reception.

If the reponse is favorable, schedule a meeting and put your offer on the table. Emphasize how serious the situation is and how favorably this offer compares with the contracts at competing firms. Hammer home the notion that this is an offer born out of crisis, not necessarily what is best in the long run for everybody. In short, sell it to the bargaining committee. Be alert to the response.

Progress will still be slow. The important thing is to end the stalemate and start talking again, trying to find an answer. Once you start, there is a good chance you can reach a settlement — after a lot of work and long hours. Remember, this is going to be a salvage operation, not a work of art. Be flexible but determined.

Reach Agreement

In time, the bargaining process should yield an agreement. Try to make sure that the union's leadership will recommend ratification and will work for it. It is the union's job to sell the contract, but you can be helpful by permitting balloting on the company's premises, allowing workers to return to work before formal ratification, and reducing mention of disciplinary measures. Do not gloat over any concessions the union had to make and ignore any signs of union glee over your concessions. That's part of winning ratification. Indeed, it's a good rule not to comment publicly on any part of a tentative contract; you can only hurt yourself. Just be happy to have it done and welcome a return to work.

Prepare for the Next Round

As soon as ratification is complete and the agreement safely on the shelf, it is time to start planning for the next round of talks. Decide where you want to be at that time and put together a program for getting there. After a cooling-off period, start the preparation with the union's leadership and keep the next round in mind as you make decisions affecting your business.

Your labor cost objectives should be a major factor in plant-site selections, subcontracting, introduction of automation, amount of labor designed into new products, inventory levels, budgeting, quality planning and control, and examination of competitive plants and processes. Gear up early to be more competitive, and the next negotiations will be much easier.

THE HOSTILE TAKEOVER

The telephone rings and there is a familiar voice on the line. "Harry, this is Joe Brown from National, Inc. We've been buying your stock recently, and I want to ask your cooperation in getting our two companies together. We'll be notifying the SEC tomorrow of our intentions to tender for a sizable percent of your shares for the purpose of an eventual takeover. We'll offer twenty percent over market value — all in cash. What do you say? Shall I drop over and see you this afternoon, say at four-thirty, after the market has closed?"

The attack comes completely out of the blue. You have no defense plan in place. The offer is ridiculously low, but your stock is undervalued by the market and your shares are held mostly by institutions and pension funds that care about nothing but getting a better price. You are convinced that your shareholders will be damaged badly if the offer is accepted because you project far better results than the stock market currently reflects.

Repel the Attacker

Buy time. Tell Joe Brown that he is in for a hell of a fight. Refuse to meet with him and refuse him access to anyone in your organization. Get off the phone and get going.

Assemble Your Team

Convene your most senior people and tell them what's happened. Form a response team and pass out assignments. Your legal, financial, and public affairs people will have to get into action especially fast. Tell them to clear their desks of everything else and be prepared to meet almost continuously for the duration of the crisis. Call your board members to fill them in and explain why you oppose the raid; alert them that a special meeting may be called on short notice.

Activate Specialists

Bring in your investment bankers, outside special legal help, and public relations advisers to assist you and your people. Develop tactical options for the next seventy-two hours.

Consider the Offer

If after further examination you conclude that a marriage would be a good one for the stockholders *at the right price* and that there is no deal stopper, then you will be in the enviable position of simply maneuvering for the best possible figure. Your investment bankers will be very important here, and their advice on what you are worth will suggest the tactics you should follow.

Reject the Offer

In the more likely case that the attack is hostile, grossly inadequate, and destructive to shareholder and other constituency interests, the bid should be rejected and counteractions begun.

Inform Your Public

Notify your shareholders by newspaper and tell employees, lenders, and suppliers of the attack and of the detrimental effects on their interests — and of your intention to fight the assault. Establish methods for reporting additional information as the crisis unfolds.

Invoke Protection

Even though you should have acted before, it is still not too late to protect your company from a predator. With your outside counselors and investment bankers, develop a program of defense. Among the options are:

- Shark repellents: staggered board terms, supermajorities, reincorporation, by-law changes, lockups
- Stock repurchases or self-tenders
- A white knight
- Debt assumption and debt limitations
- Regulatory delays or denials
- Legal technicalities
- Self-offered leveraged buyout

- Personal attacks on the predator
- Greenmail
- Crown jewel divestment
- Poison pills
- Scorched-earth policy
- Pac-Man counteroffer

Use whichever of these is appropriate to protect your stockholders and is legitimate. The last five are not ordinarily recommended.

Gather Friends

This is the time to use your network. Cooperative banks might be persuaded to limit funds to the attacker. They can also be a source of funds to drive up the price of your stock and make you less appealing to an attacker.

An interested company might be willing to be a co-defender, either as a white knight or as the buyer of your attacker. There is no limit to the things you can try with the right network and a good investment banker. Such people will help only if there is something in it for them, of course, but that's to be expected.

Exhaust Your Attacker

By containing the initial attack, you have bought time. Surprise and momentum will no longer be your attacker's advantages. You must seize the advantage yourself with your response. Grind your enemy down; he won't like a prolonged battle. If your access to resources is rich and you are just as smart, you can prevail. Otherwise, you'll have to make a difficult choice. Most companies fall into the arms of a white knight if they can't mount a successful defense.

Win

Hold out until the attacker is subdued, distracted, or disenchanted. Occasionally it happens.

Eliminate the Attraction

Change whatever it was that invited the attack. Your company was viewed as being undervalued if your stock price was too low, so get it up to where it belongs! Take on debt, repurchase stock, increase dividends — build market value. If you have excess cash, invest it in hard-working assets, self-tenders, or in some useful restructuring.

Set Up a New Defense Plan

When it is all over, prepare for the next attack. Establish your defense plan and ensure that your market value is recognized.

ADVERSE INTERNATIONAL EVENT

The government in your best overseas market has just collapsed. The previous ruler, so friendly to the United States, has been overthrown in a popular revolt. The new government is intensely hostile. Trade has been cut off, and your operations in the United States that are dependent on trade with the country have been suspended because of the uncertainty. How do you handle the upheaval?

Understand the Causes

Find out what underlies the political change and what it portends. Tap experts in the State, Treasury, and Commerce departments for their interpretations. Consult with academics and others familiar with the country to get a feel for what is likely to happen. Inquire at multinational banks with listening posts in the area. Assess what is going to happen in the next sixty days and protect your exposed assets.

Collect all your receivables; divert shipping from the country; and suspend payables until more is known.

Determine the Gravity

Piece together all the information and draw up three outlines. First, lay out the most likely sequence of events. Then sketch a best case and a worst case. Be quite specific about your assumptions and what actions each case suggests.

Reach conclusions concerning the gravity and duration of the crisis and then act on the most likely possibility. Continue thinking about the worst case, but avoid taking irreversible actions on worst-case assumptions; they can be very costly.

Move Swiftly

Pull together a sixty-day plan, and move fast. Fortunes have been lost overnight. Check with other firms caught in the same circumstances to confirm your direction. The losses from inaction can be more severe than the cost of overreaction.

Take the Long Look

Having stabilized your situation, go back to your intelligence sources for additional readings. Determine the changes that will affect your business and how you can better manage matters to save at least some of your operations.

Try a pilot shipment to the country when the climate seems to have improved. Perhaps a local agent can get things going. Your product may be viewed as necessary for the public welfare or for defense. Maybe it can be shipped in from a neutral country. With the passage of time, you may find oblique methods to maintain trade with the country — if State and Commerce and Justice departments approve.

Be Patient

When a foreign market abruptly closes, your best tactic is patience, especially if the cause is political upheaval. You should pursue whatever legal options are available, but be prepared for an indefinite hiatus. In the meantime, conserve your resources and go after other markets.

Return to the Market

Stay close to developments. As soon as there is an opportunity, run for it. Beat your competition back into the market. You may wind up in a stronger position than you were in before. Conditions change, and you have to be poised to take advantage when they do.

REGULATION AND DEREGULATION

Your company is in an industry that has been relatively free of government regulation from the beginning. Now consumer groups and social activists have convinced the media and legislators that your past actions show you to be greedy, callous, insensitive, and neglectful of consumers' safety. Their solution is to regulate your products; they want agencies established to devise and enforce the regulations. What can you do?

Assess the Changed Climate

The first thing to do is take a step backward. Look at yourself in a different light. You are in a new world, and there is no point in denying it. Find out what caused the change and how far it is likely to go. Learn the ways of the social activists and get close to your legislators and their aides, and regulators. Determine the direction of their thinking. The more you know, the better you will be able to respond. You can still run a good business within a regulated environment.

Co-opt the Power Spots

Once you know what is going on, find out which people have the power and then try to influence them. If potentially onerous legislation or regulations are being considered, get to your established contacts. Point out the impracticalities and flaws in the proposals. Suggest alternatives that avoid the bad effects.

Co-opt your regulators. Occasionally the regulations are more onerous than the regulator. Get on a first-name basis with that person and be quick to provide data that can be the basis for more favorable action. Point out the pitfalls of moving too fast or too far.

Recruit your customers, suppliers, dealers, lenders, and shareholders to help you; they may have an interest in slowing a wave of regulation and should make their views known. Similarly, you should band together with your competitors to present a united front.

Exploit the Inevitable

Devote the rest of your energy to capitalizing on the new way. Instead of expending it in opposition and anger, take a positive attitude. If a new regulation is put into effect, try to exploit it. Sell the result as a virtue to your customers. Be creative; minimize cost. Get an edge on your competitors.

Remember, the history of regulation has shown that it has ultimately been to the benefit of the regulated, not to the general public. Profits of airlines grew fat under regulation, as did those of telecommunications companies and oil drillers. Profits, like mushrooms, tend to thrive in a sheltered environment.

Change Vigorously

Redesign your organization so that it can flourish in the new atmosphere. Remember that from now on you must comply with the artificial standards of the bureaucrats as well as with the discipline of the market. Reap the rewards of regulation. You may learn to like this way better. In any event, you have no choice.

Make necessary product and organizational changes with vigor. Announce the changes and tout new products. Make a positive statement whenever you can. Show that your company is on the move to meet a changing world.

Settle Down for Tomorrow

After the first flurry, solidify your contacts with politicians and regulators. Stay abreast of the shifting priorities of changing administrators. Help shape the changes, giving advice and becoming part of the process. Above all, stay lean. You can get fat easily under the umbrella of regulation. Don't turn your business into one that could not survive a move back to deregulation.

All the foregoing suggestions can be adjusted to fit a company going through a *deregulation* crisis as well, with a shift in emphasis toward dealing with competition and free markets.

THE GENERAL APPROACH

These are descriptions of and prescriptions for the worst crises you may face. In the discussion of each one, I inserted you, the newly appointed crisis manager, at the climax. You had no advance warning nor any preparation to fall back on. Your company's world was caving in, and you had to stop the collapse.

No one is likely to contend with all of these crises and certainly not always at the worst possible point. It is useful, though, to have a set of actions to consider when you encounter any one of them.

Conditions will obviously differ in individual cases, and specific considerations will affect your approach. While the course you follow may be similar to the one suggested, it will naturally be altered to the circumstances of a particular crisis. No set of suggestions is universally applicable.

On the other hand, there are general steps that can serve as a guide to handling most crises at the climax:

1. Take charge
2. Understand the circumstances
3. Define the problem
4. Rank the options
5. Move decisively
6. Eliminate the cause
7. Prevent recurrence

CONCLUSION

The art of crisis management is in its infancy. We are a long way from having a general theory or an established practice for dealing with rapid change in business situations. However, an awakening is at hand. There is a growing fascination with a subject that has been so obvious and yet been so neglected. Business people recognize that crises in commerce are on the upswing, and there is a further recognition that the conditions that permitted this surge are likely to continue.

I have gathered my thoughts in this book and forged some practical tools for dealing with business crises. It's only a beginning, but if it provides help to others, I will feel rewarded. To the extent that it can serve as a guideline for practical business judgment, I will feel fulfilled.

Index